"I have used the knowledge in Karen's books to improve my creative output so that I can work with my ideal client—the ones that make me truly passionate to show up to work every day—all while working less and making more money."

PETER LANG, THE DESIGNER CPA

"...essential reading for any accountant who wants to stand out, think differently, and lead with confidence in a rapidly changing world."

PAUL REDMOND, RDA ACCOUNTANTS

PRAISE FOR ACCOUNTANTS, YOU ARE CREATIVE

"...incredibly well-rounded advice on building a business that thrives and a team that genuinely wants to be part of it. I'll be recommending this to every accountant I know."

JAMES ROSE, CO-FOUNDER, CONTENT SNARE

"This book flips a stereotype on its head. Karen shows accountants that creativity isn't a quirky extra: It's actually your competitive edge. Suit up and prepare to see your firm, your clients, and your own potential in a whole new light!"

ANN HANDLEY, AUTHOR OF WSJ BESTSELLER *EVERYBODY WRITES*

"In her latest book, Karen gives all accountants the permission and confidence to be creative with proven techniques to unleash their creative mindsets."

IAN VACIN, AUTHOR OF *SCALE WITH PURPOSE* AND CO-FOUNDER OF KARBON

"…helps to remove that mental block and then combines that with practical ways to be more comfortable and authentic in your marketing."

DAVID ARDEN, MAP

"If you want to grow a modern firm with impact, energy, and purpose, this is essential reading."

ANDREW PICKERING AND PETE GARTLAND, ATOMIC

"...full of stories and recommendations that will help you tap into the creativity that is hiding underneath the surface of your daily work. I hope, like I did, that you'll recognize areas where you're already being creative and push yourself just a few steps further."

JONATHAN GODWIN, CPA, CEO, FOLLOW THE WOLF

"*Accountants, You Are Creative* isn't just a title or a statement. It's Karen's battle cry."

LOGAN GRAF, CPA

"...practical, honest, and full of the kind of mindset shifts our profession desperately needs."

MIKE LIBBEY, PARTNER & COO, YBL

ACCOUNTANTS, YOU ARE CREATIVE

ALSO BY KAREN L. REYBURN

The Accountant Marketer: The Structured Approach Any Accountant Can Follow to Attract Clients They Love

ACCOUNTANTS, YOU ARE CREATIVE

HOW EMBRACING YOUR CREATIVITY LEADS TO BREAKTHROUGHS IN YOUR MARKETING, BUSINESS, AND LIFE

KAREN L. REYBURN

INTREPID
PUBLISHING

INTREPID PUBLISHING
A Division of Intrepid Literary, Inc.
New York, NY
intrepidpublishinggroup.com
intrepidliterary.com

Cover design by Morgan Krehbiel

First Edition

Paperback ISBN: 978-1-972992-03-6
Ebook ISBN: 978-1-972992-01-2
Audiobook ISBN: 978-1-972992-04-3

For Gramps, whose paintings hang in my front hall and who wrote terrible poems I love to read. You drank black coffee and lived a creative life and believed I could do anything I put my mind to. Thanks for being a fan, even before I'd done anything.

And to every accountant who isn't sure they're creative. Read on.

CONTENTS

FOREWORD

You're going to want to read this book.

But to be honest, I commend you for even making it this far. Creative? Accountants? Brought to you by the author of *The Accountant Marketer*, the book that had the audacity to tell accountants they could be marketers. Accountants! Marketers! Imagine that.

She's at it again with an even wilder claim. Accountants? Creative? Karen, I'll admit I'd feared you may have overextended your social credit line with this one.

In fact, when Karen asked me to write this foreword, I hesitated for obvious reasons. I talk with accountants every day, and while no two accountants are the same, it may not surprise you to hear creativity is not a quality accountants score themselves highly on.

But as I dove into the manuscript, amidst the Lord of the Rings and Harry Potter anecdotes (this is still Karen Reyburn, after all), I discovered some real sorcery.

The book left me convinced creativity doesn't just have a place at the company retreat between the ropes course and trust falls. In this day and age, *it's an imperative*. Not just to position yourself for professional success, but to find your personal path to fulfilment.

Algorithms have a funny way of connecting us. Karen first entered my universe with a photo from the other side of the world in a social feed, a particularly beautiful photo of the Scottish countryside. I still remember showing it to my wife: *Look at this. I think she just lives here. Can you imagine?*

The layers of serendipity in this moment, my obsession with this image, wouldn't be uncovered until years later.

Somewhere there's probably a line of code to blame for this serendipity, tapping into a deep genetic longing to return to the motherland, ultimately manifesting itself as travel ads and a thirty-day bagpipe challenge.

But I like to think it was something ordained by the universe when I connected the dots two years later:

It was the same Karen who had reshaped the firms of several of my closest friends through her marketing agency.

The same Karen who, with her last book, challenged me to rethink how I view myself as an accountant.

The same Karen who has opened a generation of accountants' eyes to how to better their practice and whose Instagram posts continue to fuel a deep amount of wanderlust.

Started from Loch Lomond now we're friends. (If you just read that line, a tremendous amount of credit goes to Karen and her literary team for allowing a Drake meme in a foreword to an accounting book. A true testament to the creativity of all involved in this process.)

Paul Graham famously said, "If you want to know who you are, look at what you do." The reason you need to read this book today is it's a practical road map to *doing* creativity, weaving it into the rhythms and habits of your life to ensure you never remove *yourself* from what you're putting into the world.

This book shows how *creativity as a practice* brings you closer to your authentic self. In a world careening towards homogenization, where machine-generated knowledge threatens to overwhelm human insight, all that remains is that which is uniquely you. Because the one thing nobody's looking for is another generic accounting firm.

My hope is Karen unlocks for you in the following pages what she has for so many of us—that what your business and your future clients are clamouring for is the bit of you that you give permission to bleed through the accounting—and that you discover how embracing creativity as a means of staying in touch with your *self* is an investment worth making.

Having been on this journey myself, I can attest that the result is a business you'll be proud of.

Jason Staats
CPA, keynote speaker, and host of the *Jason On Firms* podcast

INTRODUCTION

Accountants have come a long way from the days when everyone presumed those in the industry were all the same, and all boring. Some accountants work with audiences like creatives or gamers or writers. Some have offices with a really cool vibe (and game rooms and VR headsets and baristas) while others have skipped the office altogether and work from wherever the hell they want.

Even if you're thinking, *I'm not sure I'm* that *cool*, there's still an element of humanity you lean into which makes you different from the stereotype. Maybe you work from the Scottish Highlands and do a bit of bagpiping now and then like Karen Kennedy. Or you wear pink and published a book about overcoming obstacles and are working towards living six months of the year in Paris like Nesha Pai.

It's possible this is a new concept to you, too, and you've picked up this book because you're wondering what your humanity element is. I'll tell you: It's the fact that, as a human, you are creative. And this creativity, when you recognise it and lean into it, can change your life. Your accounting business. Even the world around you.

In spite of the fact that accountants are gloriously human and enjoyable to be around and, yes, creative . . . not everyone knows this. The stereotype is unfortunately alive and well in places and in different people. This is enhanced further by the fact that we're now in an age where we're all beginning to question whether things are human created or machine generated, so we don't even know what true creativity is anymore.

This book is about helping you know you're an accountant who is also a creative person and recognising the power this gives you to stand out as the best of yourself in a world which is beginning to ask, "Real or not real?"

I wish I could use the term "creative accountant" and not have people think it means someone who tampers with the numbers, who looks for loopholes which may or may not be illegal. But even there, the word "creative" in connection with accountants has also been taken, misused, and twisted to mean the opposite of creative good.

The simplest definition of creativity, and the one I'll use throughout this book, is a combination of problem-solving and curiosity with a rhythm of consistency. And if that is starting to sound like hard work, I've got news for you: Creativity absolutely requires work. It's similar to the entrepreneurial mindset you had to start your accounting business. The mindset came naturally, but it takes time to adjust to the day-to-day reality of being a business owner and implementing your entrepreneurial ideas. Creativity follows a similar path. You are creative, but seeing that creativity come to life in your business can take time and adjustment. It's also possible this is the first time you're truly recognising and owning the creative mindset you already have—as an accountant!

Being an accountant and being a creative person are both identities that are misunderstood. I know this because I'm a qualified accountant myself. I'm fortunate enough to have founded and run a creative agency, so it's a little easier for people to understand how the two fit together, but when I tell them we work exclusively with accountants, the stereotyping still appears. To this day, I get the same reactions when I find myself meeting someone new—at an event, staying in a bed and breakfast, hiking the hills—and they ask what I do. I tell them about my marketing agency and how we exist to help accountants with marketing, and with a confused look, they ask, "Accountants? Why? Do they really need marketing?"

They're defaulting to a presumption, a misunderstanding of who accountants are and what you do. They think if they need an accountant, they will ask a few mates and people will recommend someone and they will pick the cheapest one because accounting services are a must buy, a grudge buy. Something they have to have. If possible, they do the work themselves, but if they get stuck, they find someone who sends them a big bill for work they don't understand.

Even if they have a little better understanding of the importance of accountancy services, they're still looking at the accountants themselves in the old way. Accountants focus on the numbers, not things like graphic design and PR and the latest in video and tech (they presume). Accounting is boring, and marketing is fun. How can you market something that's so dull? Accountants aren't creative; they're rule followers, box tickers, bean counters. I studied accountancy at university, and I got the same kind of questions even then.

Them: "What are you studying?"

Me: "Accounting."

Them: "Ugh, why?! Accounting is boring. I wouldn't study that if you paid me."

At first, it annoyed me, and I didn't know what to say. After a while, I pushed back. "Well, no one is asking you to study accountancy," I'd say. "It's me that's studying it. What kind of a world is it if we all found the exact same things exciting or boring? And almost everyone needs accounting in one way or another." Even after more than twenty years of working in and with the accounting industry, I still meet people who think accountants are boring.

It is beautiful to see these presumptions about accountants being overcome, slowly, by accountants who show they are human too. There are firms like Farnell Clarke, who have a bar and a pool table in their offices. Every Friday, they open a keg from one of their clients and hand round pints while turning the boardroom table into a pool table. Firms like Ashton McGill, who took the decision on setting up the firm to ensure that their coffee was world-class, even going so far as to have an accountant who is also a barista. Firm owners like Cheryl Sharp, who started a podcast about her experiences with domestic abuse, her journey as a business owner, and what it means to believe in yourself, especially as a female business owner.

They're showing their humanity and demonstrating how their ability to be interesting and creative (and even fun) connects to those aspects of their clients' businesses too. Best of all, they believe showing who they are really does matter. What you believe about yourself as an accountant is far more important than the responses or presumptions of others. It has a direct impact on the success of your own marketing. If there's any lingering thought in your mind that accounting is boring, it's too difficult to market your firm, or you are "just an accountant," then you're forgetting you, too, are a creative person.

Accountants tell me things like:

"Well, I'm not sure what kind of images to use. I'm not a designer."

"I was wondering about doing this in our firm, but I'm no marketer."

"I'd like to write more blog posts, but accounting topics are really dry."

"Oh, I'm no good on video."

"I'm just not creative."

Worst of all, people may agree with you—*That's true, accounting is dry. Yeah, marketing isn't your thing. Nope, you're not a designer.*

Well, I'm disagreeing with you. I've worked with hundreds of accountants and connected with thousands more with my books and speaking engagements and podcasts, and I know this to be true: Accountants are incredibly creative people. And when you lean into your creativity, it opens up a world of possibility in your marketing. It provides you with new opportunities to have the kind of firm which is everything you want in a business. A firm full of clients who are people you enjoy spending time with and who you like as humans (not just business owners who pay your bills). The kind that attracts team members who reflect the values you believe are most important in life and allows them to work with clients you all enjoy working with. A place where your ideas matter and can change the course of your life.

Yes, people around you are creative: artists and writers and brewery owners and agency owners. But they're not separated from you because of what they do; their creativity isn't dependent on their outcomes. It's a human quality they've leaned into and accepted. Sure, society itself has accepted artists as creative, but creativity is not art. Ed Catmull, the CEO of Pixar and author of *Creativity, Inc.,* says, "I believe that we all have the potential to solve problems and express ourselves creatively. What stands in our way are these hidden barriers—the misconceptions and assumptions that impede us without our knowing it."

Accountants are creative too. You are creative. And knowing this will make the difference between having a decent accounting firm which ticks over well enough and having an accounting business which impacts your world and the world around you in a way that matters.

So what is creativity anyway?

SECTION ONE:

What is creativity?

1 WHAT IS CREATIVITY?

WHAT IS CREATIVITY ANYWAY?

Once when I was in London for an accounting conference, I popped into a Starbucks to get my morning coffee. (Black, please.) My agency, PF, has a series of branded shirts, and the one I was wearing is bright yellow and says "You are creative" on the front. The barista noticed the shirt while I was ordering and commented on it.

"Does that mean you are creative? Or does it mean I am creative?" he asked.

"Well, both, actually," I answered. "Every human being is creative, so it applies to everyone."

"Oh . . . I don't know about that!" He laughed a little uncomfortably. "I don't feel very creative."

"Well, if it makes you feel better," I said, "my agency works exclusively with accountants. And this shirt was originally designed to help remind them that they are creative too."

"Oh, well," he said, "if accountants can be creative, then maybe I can be."

The word "creativity" can bring up the idea of artists.

Painters. Writers. People who are creative . . . who create things. Out of nothing. The Latin *ex nihilo*: "Out of nothing, creation." As an accountant, you're not starting with a blank page. The numbers are there and need to be organised, but you're not creating them out of thin air. (That's the illegal kind of creative accountant.) Even when I was trying to define creativity, I found it difficult. Isn't the point that it's free and open and full of potential? But the more I explore creativity, the more I see that part of its beauty is how we all express it in different ways.

My mum worked as a research chemist. My dad was a computer engineer. And I studied accountancy. You can appreciate why, growing up, my mum didn't consider herself creative. She'd look at something I or one of my sisters did—a painting, illustrations in art class, photographs I'd taken at the local zoo—and say, "I don't know where you got all that creativity!"

But this same woman could make an incredible dinner from a few leftover pieces of chicken, some cheese, a sauce she whipped up, and some old dried-up potatoes. It would be mouth-wateringly good. My sisters and I would say, "This is delicious! What's in it?" and she'd say, "Oh, just some chicken and carrots and a few potatoes." I'd ask her for the recipe, and she'd say she didn't have one. Or she'd tell me the recipe, but she'd made so many edits to it that it had become something new. She'd start with a recipe for chicken pot pie but didn't have any chicken, so she'd use turkey. And there was no pastry, so she used spiral pasta. We'd be eating this turkey broccoli pasta bake, and when we asked what it was, she'd say, "Well, it's chicken pot pie, of course." It got to the point we'd be eating an apple pie and say, "Mum, this is amazing! Did it start out as chicken enchiladas?"

She was incredible in the garden as well. She'd buy a few packets of seeds, and I'd go away to university and come back four months later and wonder if I had the right house. They lived in Phoenix, in the heart of the Arizona desert, and I'd open a gate and feel like I'd arrived in a flowering corner of Greece, surrounded by potted plants and hanging vines and trickling water. The woman is one of the most creative people I know.

All humans are creative. It's in our nature. We reflect the creativity of the universe itself, a place full of sunsets and waterfalls and giraffes whose knees bend backwards and northern lights drawn across a black sky as if with an invisible hand. Just because you're not a painter or a gardener or using virtual reality tech doesn't mean you aren't creative. I see accountants writing blog posts from the perspective of the office dog. Holding parties to announce a new accounting regulation. And ideas—constant ideas. I see you exploring how you can help your clients better, how to show your team and culture and values better. Yes, a creative agency can help take the ideas you have and bring them to life or turn it into something on-brand and visually impressive, but the core idea is yours. We're both being creative in our unique ways.

Ultimately, creativity includes these two important things:

Problem-solving

and

curiosity.

(With an underlying rhythm of consistency, which we'll talk about later on in the book.)

When I meet an accountant who is eager and willing to solve problems—of whatever kind, whether it's in systems or onboarding or website or hiring—I see sparks of creativity. If you believe you're not creative, that shuts down or slows down the very qualities you need the most, those which will provide the most help to you, your business, and your whole team.

When you think about problem-solving and curiosity, it's a little easier (I hope) to believe in your own creativity. Even if you're not much for drawing or if you find it easier to work through a spreadsheet than to record a video, you can still tap into those two qualities. What's the problem here I can work on solving? How can I have a curious, open mind to ask questions and see things differently? Who could I involve in this process to help me see new possibilities and to remind me that in creativity, there's no right answer?

That's the real kicker with creativity: There's no right answer. There are no debit and credit columns that always add up. It can be a scribbly mess, like a child with crayons going all over the page and outside the lines and onto the table. Or wall. You try something. Maybe it works, and maybe it doesn't. Maybe it sort of works, but you need to tweak it a little. Maybe in the process of working on it you realise what's wrong. Maybe you can't figure it out, so you scrap the whole thing and try something else.

**That's the real kicker with creativity:
There's no right answer.**

Yes, accounting follows rules. And you help your clients do that (or you sort it out for them). But what you really love, what stirs you up and gets you motivated and keeps you doing this work you call accounting, is the conversations with your clients about their business problems. Whether it's a problem with their numbers or software or prices or products or team or taxes or lockdown or profits, you get to look at the pieces and consider what the possible solutions are. And you and your client both get to stay curious and ask new questions and get excited and find a new way (or an old way) that works.

All of that is creativity. All of that is problem-solving and curiosity.

WHAT IS THE VALUE OF CREATIVITY TO ME, THE ACCOUNTANT?

Okay, so I'm doing more of what I enjoy. And I'm helping solve problems and leaning into what I enjoy . . . but what's the true value of that? What's the return on investment (ROI) of creativity?

This question relates back to the ROI of marketing too. It's so tempting to create a "this for that" version of ROI. You think, *Okay, I sent out an email about booking a free strategy call and two people replied, so that was clearly a success.* But you posted on LinkedIn twice a week for a month, and nothing happened. You might decide LinkedIn doesn't work for you or even come to the conclusion that emails are better than social media. And yet that's not how marketing ROI truly works because there are invisible and less tangible things happening every day which affected the apparent success (or failure) of your email or social posts.

Determining the value of creativity isn't a tidy little formula I can provide, like saying five minutes of creative time every week equals a 5 percent increase in your revenue. But as with all things marketing, the question about ROI involves determining what success means to *you*. Do you want to write a book? Get more speaking engagements? Spend fewer hours on the day-to-day of the business? Have fewer video meets and more time with your family?

Applying a creative mindset to achieving those goals changes things and gives you an insight into the value of creativity. You might be thinking, *Yes, yes, if I do what I've always done, I'll get what I've always gotten.* But the truth is more like "If you do what you've always done, you'll get less." Because the rest of the world is moving forward as fast as they possibly can. This isn't a rallying cry to hustle culture; section 4 of this book addresses the power of rest to help your creativity. Instead, this is a reminder that innovation comes from creativity. It doesn't come from doing things the same way you've always been doing them. If you have goals you want to achieve, especially if those have been proving challenging to achieve lately, building your creative skills will help you achieve those—but it may not be in the way you expect.

As an accountant, you take pride in the internal functions of running your accounting firm. The systems, the processes, the profits. You can find yourself focusing on the technical aspects of what you do as an accountant and what you consider impressive. But the value of creativity also involves being able to see your firm from the perspective of the people you serve. When you truly look at things from the client's perspective, you begin to have a very different view of what your firm is and what these systems are for. Most accountants love a good spreadsheet, but your clients don't care about that. They love what it can do for them, what it delivers in their business and their life. The more they value your firm, the more services they will need, and the more they'll be willing to pay for those services too.

There's another area of your accounting firm impacted by creativity, and that's the culture and attitude of your team. How you create and deliver your marketing affects the kind of clients you get; it also impacts the kind of team members who apply to work with you and stay with your firm. We're no longer in a time when being an accountant or bookkeeper means sitting quietly in a corner, speaking to nobody, being best friends with the adding machine. The true value in the accountant is in the advice you give your clients, the way you interpret the numbers, and the impact of the relationship on their business and life. Sure, some team members will be less client-facing than others, and there will still be those who prefer a more introverted life or a quieter working environment. But the younger generation of accountants often want more—and not necessarily more money. They want more time, more freedom— and, yes, more creativity. Room to try things, explore systems, work with different kinds of clients. So the firms who are attracting the best accounting talent are those who are providing room for their team members' creativity too.

The true value in the accountant is in the advice you give your clients, the way you interpret the numbers, and the impact of the relationship on their business and life.

The more you understand and apply the principles of creativity in your life and your firm, the better and faster you'll achieve your goals, the better and more long-lasting your relationships with clients will be, the more services they'll need from you (and the more they'll pay for those services), and the better team members you'll attract. Doesn't that sound valuable?

Those are, of course, long-term wins for you and your firm. What about the short-term wins? What can you get today, tomorrow, or this week to feel the early impact of your creativity?

That one is a little harder, but let's look back at our definition of creativity: problem-solving and curiosity with a rhythm of consistency. We'll talk more about rhythms in section 4, but it can feel a bit backwards to focus on rhythms and patterns in connection with creativity. Surely you're meant to fling things around, try something new every day, go wild? Good news—or at least I'm presuming this is good news for most accountants reading this—it's really the hard work and consistency that bring out your innate creativity. Even in the short term, showing up at the same time every day with the same focus can change things. The difference is you're not determining ahead of time what it's going to change. You're leaving it open. The change could relate to sales or your team, and it could also have an impact beyond your business, on your headspace or your physical health.

If you'd like to start seeing a creative impact as soon as possible, I recommend this exercise:

- Pick one area, like video or writing or running or using new tech.
- Choose a set amount of time you can reasonably commit to every day (like five minutes or twenty minutes).
- Ideally, choose the same time of day every day.
- Show up during that time, for that length of time, to work on that area. Record a video or write a set number of words or run or try a new kind of AI.

When you do this, there will be some kind of result. Cheryl Sharp started by recording regular Instagram reels and began adding them to YouTube as shorts. "Engagement and viewers exploded," she told me. "I was getting one or two views, and now I'm getting five hundred, seven hundred views at a time." Paul Redmond completed the 100-day video challenge (I'll explain more about this later in the book) and afterward noticed he had more leads coming into the practice than ever before. He said, "Previously, I would have had maybe two leads a year for business acquisition. I got five leads in the past week.

I attribute it to being out there, being prominent. People are looking for help, and they remember you're there."

However, the result which stood out the most for both Cheryl and Paul was not a financial one. Paul told me, "The video which got the most feedback and engagement was the one in which I shared about getting cancer. My wife got cancer after I did, so we were going through it at the same time. I got the most amazing message from someone I didn't know, someone I'd never met, to say how much my one video helped them. That alone made it worth doing the entire challenge."

For Cheryl, it was a mindset shift. "I was fine with recording video, but reels felt different," Cheryl said. "I thought of them as the fun ones—the dancing, the lip syncing, the silly stuff. That wasn't my comfort zone. So because I didn't enjoy those, but I saw others doing them, I thought I was rubbish. Now, I am empowered. I know the kinds of reels I like to do and the ones I don't. The pressure is gone."

Both Cheryl and Paul initially sought to exercise their creativity. They wanted to do something that was challenging or new and show up in a way they were proud of. You'll read more about their stories later in this book, but there are hundreds of similar stories I could tell of accountants who took even the smallest step to lean into their creativity and saw an impact they weren't expecting. I won't be able to guarantee what your return looks like, but if you are consistent and stick with it, I can reasonably guarantee there will be some kind of result. Something will happen—and many times, it may be something you didn't expect. That's the beauty of creativity's ROI: It's surprising.

Now, let's look at the impact creativity can have on your firm's marketing and on you personally.

SECTION TWO:

Why it matters & how it impacts your marketing

2 WHY IT MATTERS AND HOW IT IMPACTS YOUR MARKETING

Believing you are creative impacts your firm, but before we look at your firm's results, we need to look at your identity.

YOU PERSONALLY

Owning your identity as a creative person

Even if you're already recognising the potential impact of knowing and believing you're creative, you'll be tempted to stay carefully in the realm of what feels familiar, keeping a focus on outcomes and results. You might remember having tried something you consider creative and feeling like it was a fail. Perhaps you even stuck at it for longer than before—you wrote a blog post every week or started posting on LinkedIn every day—but got disappointed by the lack of results. This is a good opportunity to consider the interconnectedness of three things: outcomes, systems, and identity.

Outcomes are *what you get*: better clients, more sales, higher profits.

Systems are *what you do*: consistent content creation, recording videos, writing down client questions.

Identity is *what you believe about yourself*: I am a writer. I am curious. I am creative.

Without embracing the identity, you'll always default to a focus on results or the systems which worked before (or you thought they did). You stop asking questions, settle into your old patterns, and focus on your old accountant identity.

I'm not a runner, but I love the idea of it. The people I know who are runners have aspects to their identity which I like and am inspired by. I love how many of them get up early in the morning while it's still dark and see the sun rise as they go on their morning run. Or the way they go from running a 5K to running a 10K to running a marathon to running an ultramarathon. My sister runs ultras so often they're just something she does. I'll be staying with my family for Christmas and come bleary-eyed into the kitchen for coffee, only to see my sister appearing at the front door, bright-eyed and shining.

"How far did you go?" I mumble as I try to find the coffee pot.

"Only ten miles," she sings, practically dancing her way to the counter. I groan a little and think maybe I'll walk a mile or two later.

I've tried multiple times to get into running. There have been several times in my life when I remember texting this same sister with great excitement because I actually felt like running. I walk every day, but it was as if walking wasn't enough—I needed to go faster, and I could, and I was off! Hurrah! *Perhaps I'll be a runner after all*, I'd think. Every time, something would happen. One time, it was shin splints. Another time, my back was a bit sore, and the next weekend, I was carrying something heavy and—*twang!*—there went my back, and I wasn't walking or running or really moving very much for three months. Every single time I've attempted running, without fail, I've experienced an injury not long after which has made running either difficult or impossible, and it's had a huge impact on future motivation to run. My sister still believes it's possible for me because *she's a runner*. Of course, it's possible for me to be one too. I just have to try again or in a different way or at a different time in my life.

But despite being impressed with the concept of being a runner, I don't own the identity of being one. I'm a walker; that's my vibe. I love walking. I'll walk for hours or days. I'll default to it. I don't love hiking, but I'll do it to get to beautiful places, and I like hikes with a combination of walking and climbing rather than the sheer, endless climbs without a straight path to be seen. But if I have a choice and there's a path in front of me, I'll choose walking. I remember one time walking for over an hour and a half to an appointment in Edinburgh rather than taking a bus route I didn't understand. Walking was easy. It's my favourite way to get places. I'm a walker.

If I were to try again with running, I'd need to own *all three* of the aspects of running: the systems, the outcome, and the identity. A runner wouldn't stop because of an injury. Well, they'd stop for a short while, and then they'd start again and not just because they have a habit of running or because they bought the right shoes. It's because *they are a runner*, right down to their soul, and they know it.

You can build rhythms of creativity, and we'll look at those in section 4. You can even see some results from practising it in your life and work. But it will have the greatest impact—and bring you the greatest outcomes—when you embrace your identity as a creative person. *I am creative*. You're not an accountant playing with creativity or trying it as a habit for a few months and then going back to other things. You're a creative person stirring up a latent quality, something which has been obscured and hidden for years. Best of all, it's not like the process I'd need to make to go from being a walker to a runner. It's not a new identity for you to consider whether you want it; it's already there. You are creative. It exists within you. It's a matter of reminding yourself of this fact and noticing the indicators of it in your life.

You are creative. It exists within you. It's a matter of reminding yourself of this fact and noticing the indicators of it in your life.

Question everything

Part of the curiosity aspect of creativity is to *question everything*. It brings to mind the small child whose endless question of "Why?" is both utterly fascinating and, some days, teeth-grittingly annoying. My mum would patiently endure an almost endless succession of "why" questions from me or my sisters—until she reached the point of defaulting to the parental right of saying, "Because I said so," and that ended the conversation. At least, it ended the conversation with her. Nothing prevented us going to someone else—a sibling, another parent, a grandparent—and continuing the never-ending procession of whys.

Asking "why" is good, and asking a "what" version of the question is even better, especially when you're asking someone else. If you tell me you're buying a new house and I ask, "Why?" you will explain all the reasons why moving is so great, and you might feel a little defensive about your decision. Perhaps I think moving isn't a good idea or I believe your current house is amazing, and I'm asking why because I disagree with you. If instead I respond with "Oh wow! What led you to the decision to move?" or "What do you love about your new house?" there's more openness and a greater variety to the direction the conversation can go. A why question insists on there being a reason and usually one reason above all that must be defended. A what question leaves room for curiosity, openness, and many reasons.

Children ask why because they tend to be looking for an answer, a reason for something they don't understand. As creative adults, we ask questions to explore, to understand many options, and to recognise the presented solution may not be the solution. We can ask questions in a variety of ways, but the important thing is to ask the questions. You've decided to start blogging as your creative exercise—why? What was appealing to you about that particular action? Was there another one you considered but rejected? What if there's another one still better?

In the film *Dead Poets Society*, the teacher Mr. Keating is explaining to his students the value of seeing things from another perspective. He jumps up on the big desk at the front of the classroom and asks the class why he's standing up there.

One of the students jokes that he's doing it to feel taller, and all the other students laugh.

"No!" Keating says, ringing the small bell on his desk with his foot. He tells them he stands upon his desk to remind himself we must constantly look at things in a different way.

He stands there for a moment, turning to observe the room, the paintings, and the students. Things look very different from up there. He invites the students to come to the desk and stand on it themselves. Some do so quickly, enthusiastically. Some are nervous, wondering if this is okay, if it's right to be standing on a teacher's desk in a classroom.

"Just when you think you know something, you have to look at it in another way," he says as they step up, stand on the desk, look around, and then jump down. "Even though it may seem silly or wrong, you *must* try," he tells them. "When you read, don't just consider what the author thinks. Consider what *you* think. Boys, you must strive to find *your own voice* because the longer you wait to begin, the less likely you are to find it at all."

I give this same advice to you, the accountant. Just when you think you know something, especially about content creation or lead generation or social media or any of these marketing aspects, it's time to look at it in another way. Is there another perspective you can consider? Another book or article you can read? What questions can you ask of yourself, of an expert, of a client?

Sometimes merely changing your environment is a helpful way to question everything. Any time you've moved house (or cities or countries, even), you'll experience this. When I started my agency, I was working from a corner table in the second bedroom of my flat. After a few years, I bought a bookcase and a bigger desk and set up a whole space for working. A few years more, and I moved house and had an entire room dedicated to my home office. The change in approach and in mindset is no coincidence; each time I moved, I had the opportunity to pause and ask, "What do I *want* my working environment to look like? How and where and when do I do my best work?" Even if you're not in the middle of a move (or if you feel stuck in a tiny or ugly place), you have options about where you sit or what table you use or where you do your writing. Questioning everything may mean standing on a table for a moment and looking around the room differently.

Creativity Exercise

Pick a different chair in the room you usually work in or move your desk for a different view. Work from there for a day and see what difference it makes to your mindset.

YOUR FIRM: SERVICE DESIGN

"Service design is a new concept, but it is grounded in good old common sense," says Alasdair McGill, an accountant with over twenty years' experience in what's called service design: a way of thinking about how you deliver your services so you make life easier for your clients as you help solve the problems they're facing. When we have an experience we love, it's often because the owners or those who built the experience thought about how you and everyone else might feel and crafted things accordingly. Going paddleboarding with a group? It stands to reason some within the group will be more experienced and some less. Wouldn't it make sense for a company providing the paddleboarding to record videos for each experience level and send them a few weeks ahead so everyone feels comfortable and ready and enthusiastic?

Not everyone does it, though. Too often services are either delivered the way the person providing them finds best, so it's focused on them and not on the recipient, or they're delivered the way they've always been delivered without anyone stopping to think if that's still the best way or if it ever has been. Think about the last time you encountered something which was slightly different and better than you expected. Think about the first time you put your name in for a table at a restaurant and were handed a small beeper that would buzz when your table was ready so you could wander around the area and come back. You'd thought about how frustrating it would be to wait around with everyone else, but you hadn't thought about a different way to do it until you saw it in practice.

Applying creativity to the marketing of your firm doesn't mean you're coming up with ways to *make* people buy from you. You're thinking of new ways to show who you truly are, what you're really like, and how you really help people. This way, you don't have to explain it over and over—you can let your marketing do that for you. Those two aspects of creativity, problem-solving and curiosity, when applied to the way you do things in your firm, will help you design and deliver not only services but an *experience*. This means starting by considering how people feel when they connect with you and other members of your firm.

You can consider their feelings at every stage of the connection. How do they feel when they encounter your website? When they fill in the form or request a call? What about in the days before the meeting, during the meeting itself, and afterward? What about when they've got the proposal? The more you consider their emotions, the more you can use service design to craft the experience in a way they will find comfortable, pleasant, and one they wish to repeat. Your number one focus is how you can make life easier for your clients, including before, during, and after they become a client.

Peter Shankman, in his book *Nice Companies Finish First: Why Cutthroat Management Is Over—and Collaboration Is In*, says the expectations of customer service are often so bad that in order to wow people, all you need to be is "one level above crap." I think of this every time I fly somewhere. On the one hand, I'm amazed and grateful that I can literally cross continents in the space of a day. In the morning, I'm at home in rainy Scotland, gathering my things, and in the evening, I'm walking with my sister in the deserts of Arizona with cacti and dust all around me. On the other hand, having flown back and forth between the UK and America for over twenty years on top of other domestic and international flights for holidays and conferences and events, I also go into it fully expecting the experience to be pretty miserable. The efforts to fit everything into a certain size of suitcase. Checking to be sure any bottles in the bag I'm taking through security are the right size and checking whether they're in a specific size of clear plastic bag. Standing in queues to drop off my bag, then walking for ages and standing in more queues to go through security, then more queues to get on the plane and off the plane. Waiting for my suitcase to come round the little suitcase roundabout. Lifting my small case to fit in the extremely tiny space above my head on the plane. Having to put it further away from my seat than I intended because the plane is full, and when we arrive, standing bent over above my seat, waiting for half the plane to disembark so I can walk a few steps back and get my case. Tiny drinks which spill easily. Bland snacks everybody takes but nobody likes. Endless announcements, all of which end by telling me to sit back and relax and enjoy my flight, which I'd like to do, except my relaxation keeps getting interrupted by announcements.

And yet, when all of these (and many more) things happen during my travels and I finally arrive tired, sweaty, having been bumped and run into for hours all day with no sleep and no fresh air, and my family asks, "How were the flights?" I usually answer with "Yeah, not too bad, actually!" Because my expectation is that the entire experience will be pretty crap. When it is, that's how it was meant to be, so I don't expect any better. I'd be utterly shocked if there were loads of space and comfort, everyone was lovely and helpful, and every person I encountered sought for ways to make my life easier along the way. Granted, I could pay exorbitant amounts for a different experience, and then my expectations would change. Our expectations match the way things usually work and the way most people experience a service.

This is the kind of expectation many business owners have when they enquire about working with you as their new accountant. They have expectations about how accounting works, how taxes work, how accountants themselves work.

Many of them have had poor experiences. They've contacted their accountant endlessly with no response, they've waited for ages to finally discover they owe quite a lot of money, or they don't understand half of what the accountant tells them, and they figure it's their own fault. *Anything* which raises their expectations above the level of crap will pleasantly surprise them. And if you go beyond that, bringing them to a point where they actually enjoy the experience of meeting with you, they'll think, *You are amazing. This is incredible. I never knew it could be this way.*

The good news for most of you is this is something you're already doing. You're already considering how you can make your clients' lives easier, how you can listen to their feelings, how you can help solve their problems. Design is based on an experience lived out by people, and the people to listen to are those you serve. How can you listen? People love to talk about themselves. As you prepare your processes and systems for every aspect of your business, remember to include spaces for your clients to talk and for you to listen.

Applying service design thinking means breaking down the experience in a way that reflects the client, not you. Instead of making a list of all your services and creating processes for each one, start by thinking about the order in which someone experiences your firm.

Before they meet you: The person is in the marketing and pre-qualifying stages. They're finding your website, reading your social media posts, watching your videos. They don't know who you are yet, and their expectations of your firm relate back to the industry as a whole. They've got all kinds of emotional baggage from past experiences, and the only thing they're certain of is this will probably not go well in at least one, if not several, ways. Their feelings of suspicion and expectations of frustration are high, and the tiniest thing that doesn't go well will feed into those feelings. The easier you make things at this stage, the faster they will move into the enquiry and proposal stages.

The beginning of the relationship: Having moved through the previous stage with surprisingly little trouble and some hope about how this might be different from what they expected, they've signed the proposal and are beginning the client relationship. The way you start this relationship is the way it continues, so expectations matter even more at this stage. What are they anticipating will happen, in a positive way? What did you promise? How did onboarding go, and how are the first few months of this relationship? Any reason for them to wonder which things will continue happening and which will stop at some point?

During the client relationship: Service design doesn't end once they sign the proposal and are handed over to the team for their accounts and bookkeeping and tax work to tick away. They still have feelings, problems, issues, questions, circumstances they've never experienced before. Most of those experiences are familiar to you and your team, but the way you support your client helps them feel they are the one who matters the most at this point, because they do. When something major and significant happens—such as the opportunity to be on a live TV show, which has happened for more than one client of some accountants I've spoken to!—the way their accountant relates to them and helps them navigate the opportunity matters. At this stage, your service design considers how you respond during what's expected (the planned events) and the unexpected (when things go wrong).

After the relationship: Service design honestly recognises that at some point, people may need to leave. It could be a positive reason for the business owner; they retire or sell their business or grow it to a point well beyond your firm's experience, which requires a different level of support. If someone needs to end the client relationship, make this easy for them too. You can still include a good conversation, questions about your service and their experience, and a full understanding about why they needed to go whilst making that process as simple as possible for the leaving client. Think about how awkward and uncomfortable it is to leave some (particularly bigger) companies, such as ending your mobile phone contract. You signed up in a matter of minutes with an online form, but in order to cancel, you need to call a number and talk with a human who will try to convince you not to leave. Finding the number itself isn't easy, nor is the length of time you wait on hold. There are barriers every step of the way. They've put those barriers in on purpose, to make it hard for customers to leave, and in one sense, they're successful. Many people stay with their phone company because of the huge effort required to cancel. But that's not true success because it stirs up even more annoyance than you already had, and the reputation of the company suffers. Part of service design means you consider every stage of the client relationship, right down to the leaving part. Get comfortable with people needing to leave. Make the process and the conversation simple—for you and for them. And make room for learnings about how the process went so you can discover the kind of changes you can make which will improve the experience for every other client who doesn't need to leave.

Do good work: Right down to the detail

"If a thing is worth doing, it's worth doing well," my grandmother would say. This got passed down to my mum and then to me and my sisters. My sisters and I would sometimes respond to this attempted motivation with "Well, then it's not worth doing!" We did discover, to our disappointment, that we were not the ultimate decision-makers about the worth of the task. Something like cutting the grass or washing the dishes was worth doing in my mum's eyes, so it needed to be worth doing in ours.

Detail work is something accountants do particularly well. Sometimes it's the detail that distracts you from the bigger picture of not only what you're trying to achieve but also who you're trying to be. But as you lean into your own creativity, you can use this tendency for detail to help you practise doing good work in every tiny part of your business.

Alasdair McGill, mentioned at the start of this section, applied service design when he started an accounting firm. He had worked for twenty-five years in service design and ran a golf pro shop as well. These qualities and experiences meant he was intentional about building a firm which was good in every detail. He wanted to go beyond the typical details of a good onboarding process or an online project management system ticking boxes for each client. Alasdair and his son, Andy, wanted to build a firm which included the best details of every good accounting firm and was missing the worst details from every bad firm. To do this, they surveyed over a hundred people with one question: "What do you really *not* like about accountants or accounting firms?"

The answers were their manual for how not to build a firm. People told them they were disappointed how hard it was to get a hold of their accountant, so Alasdair and Andy built a response system to get their clients a reply to an enquiry within an hour or two at the most. Business owners reported it was discouraging that every time they wanted to try something new, their accountant defaulted to the negative or the danger. The new firm owners talked about how to infuse positivity, enthusiasm, and energy into every part of client conversations. Even if the answer ultimately was no, the team members were taught to respond to new ideas with "That's really exciting! I'd love to hear more about it" rather than "Oh, I don't think that's a good idea." People likened going to the accountant like going to the dentist, so the new firm was full of things people love, like *good* coffee and comfortable armchairs with good views out the window and local food sourced for lunches and cheerful prints on the walls. And it worked. Once they started the firm, they'd find their clients showing up at their offices to say hello and enjoy the good company of interesting people even if they didn't have an appointment to talk about their accounts that day.

The details of your clients' accounts and taxes matter, especially to you, but the details of their lives feel more important to them and need to be accounted for. What's the point of running a business if not to make your life better in some way? If the tiny, detailed improvements you make in your business affect the feelings and motivations of your clients in their businesses, they'll associate these positive feelings with your firm.

Question everything about how you do business, right down to the detail. What music do you play in the office? Do you have an office? Do you *need* offices? What days do you work? What hours during those days? Are pets allowed in the office? Do you take an afternoon walk or an afternoon siesta? So many of the presumptions we make about business and life are either cultural or simply habitual. Don't merely look at how other accounting firms do things; look at how other businesses you admire do things. Look at coffee shops, whisky distilleries, soap-making factories, bed and breakfasts, tattoo shops. I know the owners of a bed and breakfast in the Scottish Highlands who, when they visit a B&B as guests in another area of Scotland, literally take notes on what that other B&B did well or didn't do so well. What teas and coffees do they have in the room? What kind of hairdryer? What are the bedside tables made out of? How does breakfast work, and what's on the menu? How are the tables placed in the breakfast room? What soaps are in the bathroom? They take what they learn and make seemingly infinitesimal changes to their rooms, and as a result, their place is full of many good, small things. They use a local soap, shampoo, and conditioner in the showers. Their showers are better than my own at home. The breakfast is made with locally sourced ingredients from nearby farms and shops. I go back to the Coire Glas Guest House time and time again, bringing new people each time, because they do good work, right down to the detail.

Creativity Exercise

Pretend you're a new client signing up to work with your accounting firm. Book the meetings, sign the proposal, get the emails, experience the process to the best of your ability. When you notice something that could be confusing or frustrating, fix even one small aspect of that thing. Your next client will be grateful for it—and your systems will slowly improve.

When you do good detail work, some people will notice it. They might even take photos of it and share it and tell others about it. But equally, there will be hundreds or even thousands of people who never notice it at all. They'll only get a sense of it or understand it subconsciously. The Warner Bros. Studio Tour just outside of London features all the detail work that went into the eight Harry Potter films. Every time I visit, I'm reminded that the contents of this place weren't built as an entertainment for holidaymakers; these are the actual sets, props, and costumes used to create the films. And there is an impressive level of detail by the filmmakers and designers. Like using real Yorkshire stone for the floor of the Great Hall because when they tried a simulated kind of stone, the director didn't like the sound everyone's shoes made as they walked on it. It didn't sound real. So they paid a vast sum of money to get the real thing so it sounded genuine, an old stone hall that has existed for hundreds or thousands of years. Now when millions of visitors go to the studios on a visit, their shoes ring with authenticity, whether they realise it or not.

Quality was considered in the tiniest of details in every sketch, every model, every final piece used (or not used) in the films. For example, there are handwritten labels on every single potion bottle in Dumbledore's office. And when they needed shelves full of glass orbs for a scene, the film team made, or found, over fifteen thousand, only for the director to decide they would go full CGI instead. But they still kept the orbs and used them in other ways. There is great strength of creative character in recognising that everything has value when you do it well, even if it's not used as you expected. Instead of being disappointed and feeling like your effort was worthless, you move on quickly to a different kind of work. Nothing is wasted.

There is great strength of creative character in recognising that everything has value when you do it well, even if it's not used as you expected.

Those working on these films didn't know then that their work would be on display like this. They didn't realise it would be seen and photographed and become a source of inspiration for many years to come. They were simply doing the very best work for every scene, right down to the detail, not because everyone always sees it but because it's good and honourable in its own self. After all, as my grandmother would say, "If a thing is worth doing, it's worth doing well."

The way you design the whole service experience in your firm is also worth doing well. In your onboarding process, not everyone is going to notice or appreciate the accuracy of each little labelled image on the onboarding graphic you've had designed. Not every client will read every word of the onboarding pack you've created. But some of them will, and the work you did to make sure it was right—down to the smallest detail—means the overall impact will be stronger for every new client who is onboarded to your firm.

Julie Shipp, joint owner of the firm Blumer CPAs, explained to me the impact of creativity on the services they provide their clients. "Culturally, we work to encourage and elevate the team with the freedom to have very right-brain things because they live in their left brain," says Julie. Every week their team meets, there will be someone teaching the rest of the team about their personal creative outlet, something not work-related like cooking barbeque or playing the guitar or designing T-shirts. One creative exercise involved sending succulent plants to everyone on the team with the task of looking after them for two weeks and reporting back on the success (or lack thereof). This led to a lot of hilarious conversations and lessons on attentiveness and the difference between nurturing and over-nurturing.

This creative approach flows into the services the firm provides to their clients. One of their newer team members was working with a large agency client, and she wanted to create a new CFO service for agencies of this kind. She created everything for the service from start to finish. "It was really fascinating to watch her mind run down every possible trail to do that new work," Julie said. "She didn't have anything to lean back on. She had to create the full experience and literally create something from the mess." As with all creative projects, it felt a bit messy and bumpy in the early days, but about halfway along the route, she began to feel traction and see how this new service would impact the client. The new service ended up being so effective the owners were able to sell the agency because of the improvement to the financials and what those showed, and now the firm had a new service for other agencies too. This freedom of an open mind allowed an accounting team member to see things she wouldn't have seen otherwise.

Do the prep work

When you're doing this good work, it can be easy to get carried away with believing you're further ahead than you are. You're motivated. This new thing is *happening*! If only you could get it out in the world *today*! This might look like a new service for a particular niche of your clients, making your onboarding process better, or building a community for your clients and running events for them. Whatever it is, the IDEA has come to you (in all capitals in your brain), and you're on fire. You feel like you can't wait for everyone to see it because the moment they do, they'll want it. Your hard work will be rewarded, you'll be celebrated in the streets (or at least on LinkedIn) as a modern-day genius, and you may never have to truly work again. This is the level of enthusiasm our mind reaches to help us build something new. It's energetic. It's grandiose.

When we hit the light of cold, hard reality, it feels harsh. Almost rude. You were going to change the world! Why is a tech issue with the app holding you back? Or why is there yet another round of revisions from the designers? If only these things were sorted, you'd be telling the world about your idea *today*. But, oh well, there's nothing you can do. You've done your part. Now you need to wait.

Actually, there's a lot you can do while you're waiting. Here's a little trick I use when I have something I'm super excited to share—like a new guide or my book on pre-order or an event we're running—but it's delayed by something. The form isn't working on the website yet, or we haven't booked the venue. The developers have said, "Leave it with us," so I've done that. The trick is to think, *Okay, what if it was ready right now? What would I be doing or sending?* Imagine the website developer suddenly messaging me to say it's good to go or the book publisher gives me the thumbs up. The event venue is booked. Now what? Once I ask that question, I realise I'm not actually ready.

If it was ready, what are the social posts I'd be putting out? Is the content written, and are the images and hashtags ready? Do I have photographs or graphic design to go with the content? What emails are going out, and is the content written for those? Is the email list ready and segmented? Have I recorded the videos? When it comes to those videos, have I written the script or the key points? Are they portrait or landscape? How long will the videos be?

The problem is if I say, "Oh well, I guess I'll just wait," and park the whole thing, by the time the *thing* is ready, *I'm* not. I'm scrambling to write the post or send the email or do the other tasks I was so excited about a week ago. I've been there, and I'll guess you have too, more than once. So however delayed your big project seems to be, there are tasks you can be working on right now. You could be writing the wording for the blog post, the social media posts, the video script, the emails. You could open the social platform and start typing as if you're ready for the announcement today and suddenly realise there's another post you meant to write first or someone you meant to tag who you're not connected with yet.

By the time you work through all of these, you realise there's a lot to work on which will help you be far more ready than you were five minutes ago, when you were bemoaning how you couldn't possibly take action because you were waiting on someone or something else. This way, the moment the form is working or the event is live, you can click publish, and you're off!

Creativity Exercise

Identify one big project being held up right now by a significant task or issue. Imagine that issue was suddenly and magically fixed today. What would happen next? This will point you to something you can work on (like content for an email or a video script) today, which you can use once the bigger issue is solved.

It's okay to show your work in pieces as you go through the process. Share a few drafts of the book cover, run a poll to ask opinions on the event venue, share little sections of the guide before you share it in full. But asking the question "What would I do if they told me it was ready *right now*?" may reveal quite a few tasks you forgot about. Make it so that the moment this thing is ready, so are you.

In Austin Kleon's book *Show Your Work!: 10 Ways to Share Your Creativity and Get Discovered*, he explains the power of keeping people updated as you go along rather than waiting until the end for the big reveal. "90% of everything is crap," Kleon says. "The same is true of our own work. The trouble is, we don't always know what's good and what sucks. That's why it's important to get things in front of others and see how they react."

The fear of that 90 percent can hold you back too. If you're so consumed with whether your idea is The Next Great Thing or if "everyone" will like it, you won't take the creative time and space to explore it. Scotty Scarano, accounting firm owner and founder of the podcast *Accounting High*, resonates with the ups and downs of the creative process. Sometimes he's riding high on positive reactions and people who resonate with what he's creating, and other times there's negative feedback, which can lead to doubts. "I'd start to second-guess my instinct.

This person isn't going to like that, they're going to make fun of me and say this. I've gotten over it to a degree, but my mind does sometimes go back to thinking it's not just the one person who disagrees: It becomes everybody. No one is going to like this now." And then he finds himself in a creative slump, which he defines as healthy and okay. One minute you're at the peak of creativity, and you think it will never leave, but it slips away. The important thing, says Scotty, is not to allow that slump to prevent you from creating at all. Remember that's part of the creative process, and as quickly as it can disappear, equally quickly it can reappear.

> *Sometimes when you're in the thick of creativity, you think it will never go away. You're at the peak . . . but it slips away pretty quickly after a bad night of sleep or something happens and it triggers something else. It's elusive. Getting out of your own way is the key:* you *are not the art, you are not the creation. Separating yourself from that helps you be more creative.*
>
> *—Scotty Scarano, founder of* Accounting High *podcast*

BUILD ON WHAT IS GOOD ALREADY

It's also important to recognise creativity doesn't necessarily mean new ideas. When I sent out a survey on creativity, I asked people to tell me which accountants they considered to be creative. Multiple people suggested Paul Barnes, owner of accounting firm MAP (my agency's accountants) and also author of the foreword to my first book. Paul told me he was genuinely surprised people saw him as creative. "I'm guessing it appears we've taken the time to stand out, but I wouldn't label what we've done in that way. I think of it more as bringing what we do to the surface, bringing it to life."

Paul believes every accountant has what he calls a "world of gold" already: things your team are doing right now, today, which are valuable. People are putting money in your bank account for it, they value it, and you don't necessarily need to change it. He says, "A lot of times we think about creativity and marketing as new ideas, but I see it as the opposite. Instead of trying to change what your team are doing, what your firm is doing, you need to present it and amplify it to the world so it makes sense to people."

When you take that approach to creativity, instead of putting pressure on yourself and your team to change things, to come up with new ideas, to be different and stand out, you can turn and look at what you and the team are already doing right now that people tell you is valuable. Then you get a designer to create something to show this amazing thing in a new way. Maybe you don't know how to articulate it or display it, but you show them the process and explain what it does and how it impacts people. Then when they create a graphic and say, "How about this?" you say, "Oh my, yes, that's it!" And then you show it to people, and they say, "Wow, that's so powerful."

One of the small but powerful examples of this is a series of images the MAP team created for each of their services, showing the process they use to deliver that service. Management accounts, payroll, tax preparation, tax planning, bookkeeping—each service had its own graphic showing "what we do" (the accountants), "what you do" (the client), and "what happens if you don't" (consequence management). This came from a desire to help the clients see the impact of their actions (or lack of actions) on the timely delivery of the services they were paying for. If the client was responsible for their own bookkeeping and they didn't update it in time, the management accounts wouldn't be prepared, the information wouldn't be ready for the board meeting, and the company would suffer. When Paul shared one of these images with a roomful of accountants at an event we were running, the entire room became obsessed with these graphics. Sometimes finding the gold means getting inspiration from someone else's great idea and making it your own.

As Austin Kleon says in his book *Steal Like an Artist: 10 Things Nobody Told You About Being Creative*, anything people consider to be original usually means people don't know the original sources involved. Anything creative is simply building on what has come before. And rather than finding this discouraging (as if you'll never come up with a new idea), Kleon says it gives him hope: "If we're free from the burden of trying to be completely original, we can stop trying to make something out of nothing, and we can embrace influence instead of running from it."

Leaning into your own creativity as a leader and firm owner is one thing. Making it an integral part of how your business runs so every team member—and even every client—recognises and leans into their own creativity is another. Bringing your team along in the creativity journey is the starting point of community, which we'll talk about in the next section.

INVOLVING THE TEAM: BUILDING CREATIVITY INTO YOUR ROLE AS A LEADER

Creativity is both a solo exercise *and* a matter of community. If you rely on others to stir up your creativity, eventually there will be times they aren't there for you or are busy with their own things. Conversely, if you withdraw inside yourself and seek to be creative from your own resources only, you're missing the spark and opinions and perspective that can help keep creativity alive. Yes, there are creatives who have holed up from the world in order to create. This can work (or seemingly work) for a time. Thoreau spent two years in a cabin on Walden Pond, and his book *Walden; or, Life in the Woods* is a summary of that time. But he didn't go to this cabin to hide from life; he went to "live deliberately, to front only the essential facts of life, and see if I could not learn what it had to teach." He says, "I wanted to live deep and suck out all the marrow of life, to live so sturdily and Spartan-like as to put to rout all that was not life."

After he left the cabin, he became a surveyor, lived in community, and worked in the family business, eventually taking it over. The time you spend alone is valuable and useful, and it may even bring out some of your best work. The time you spend in community allows for other perspectives than your own. As we saw in the last section on service design, this is critical.

Think about how you felt about your own creativity before you picked up this book. Or how you're feeling about it now. Has any part of your perspective on that changed? This understanding of creativity is a journey. It takes time. Recognising how creativity plays in your role as a leader and beginning to show this by example to your team will also play out in a series of steps rather than all at once.

First, you need to believe it yourself. No amount of telling other people "You are creative too!" will make a difference if they aren't seeing it lived out in your life and role. Remember our discussion on identity—this is more than practising a creative exercise now and then. Your team needs to see those two skills of problem-solving and curiosity and connect those back to creativity. They need to see you embracing your identity as a creative person.

Next, you can incorporate small creative exercises into the fabric of your firm. This could be as small as five minutes at the start or end of a team meeting, or you could replace an entire team meet with a creative exercise. Start with something small that relates directly to the work your team are already doing, like writing down questions they have been asked by clients in the past week—questions they've been asked again and again—and which can lead to a list of marketing content. It's something they can do easily, and it has the potential to stretch their minds about how they think of their role and the clients they serve.

I remember doing this exercise with a team of accountants in Ireland. We were sitting around the boardroom table—seven team members, two partners, and me. The partners wanted to involve the team in marketing and had shared with me they weren't sure how to do this since the team might feel uncomfortable about something so far outside their skill sets or the requirements of their roles. I started by asking each team member how they would feel if, right now, they were suddenly asked to add marketing to their list of job requirements. We went round the table, and the answers were honest:

"Scared."

"Nervous."

"Confused."

"Like I don't know what to do."

"Wondering how I fit it in with everything else I have to do."

A few people were intrigued and said they'd feel both nervous *and* intrigued.

I said, "Okay, let's park that for now, and we'll come back to it later. What if I asked you to tell me a question a client has asked you in the past week or so which you've been asked before?"

The answers came thick and fast. There were questions about payroll, tax deadlines, forms to fill in, numbers to provide, and company types. I asked if they could give me the top bullet points of an answer to that question, and each person found that easy to do.

"Congratulations!" I told them. "You've just done marketing." I explained that although marketing can include social media posts, website builds, rebranding, and videos, those are merely the vehicles of marketing. The ideas, the content, come from the people who do the work and know the clients: these accountants sitting before me. "We can write a blog post for you," I said, "or create a new website page. But if what goes into that post or on that page doesn't come from your clients and the way you serve them, then it's not good marketing. It's just professional-sounding words."

We went round the table again to talk about how they felt now. Within that short time frame, most of the team had gone from feeling nervous and confused about marketing to feeling a little excited, relieved, motivated, and even proud. They were getting to be part of the marketing of the firm without having to become marketing experts. They had been reminded they *already were* experts in their area of accounting; their involvement in marketing was a matter of downloading what they knew and creating ways to share it with the kind of clients they wanted to work with.

Another creative exercise you can do is identifying these types of clients. Your team are the ones working with clients day in, day out. The happier they are with this type of client, the better they feel about their job, the more they enjoy their work, and the more motivated they are when given another client to work with. Conversely, if they're working with a client (or more than one client) who is difficult, frustrating, or a bad communicator, it makes their work life harder, and their motivation decreases.

Creativity Exercise

Take ten minutes in your next team meet to ask the team who their absolute favourite client is that week. What happened in the week that caused them to feel like this client was their favourite? What qualities did that client demonstrate with their actions?

One accounting firm owner, Stephen, told me about a client who was making his and the team's lives miserable. The business owner would show up late for meetings and expect to have the whole team's attention for the full amount of time. He didn't provide records on time. He yelled and got angry. When the phone rang in the office, some members of the team would actively avoid answering it in case it was *that one client.* The problem Stephen had was this person's business was a huge part of the firm's revenue, nearly 40 percent. Even though the client grumbled and shouted and made everyone miserable, they kept him on as a client because of the fees he brought in. It all came to a head one day when the owner demanded (not requested) that Stephen and the team do all the accounting for another new business he had just created, and he wanted it done within days, not weeks or months. He wanted them to set aside everything else they were working on to focus on his new venture. Stephen said he'd look at it, sent the owner away, and sat down at his desk. He realised this was their opportunity to draw the line; he could say, "No, we're not able to do this, especially within the time frame you've requested, and now we think about it, we're going to part ways." He knew the team would be thrilled this client was gone. He also knew it could have a big impact on the firm with this loss of revenue. They discussed it as a team and decided to take the consequences. They believed the energy and time currently going into this difficult client could be repurposed more profitably with other, newer clients whose values better aligned with those of the firm. So Stephen wrote the letter and told the client they were ending the relationship. The owner threw a fit. He yelled. He threatened. He disagreed. But they held firm and parted ways, and that was that.

The next morning, Stephen came into the office and noticed the entire place was *happier*. People were smiling, saying "Good morning!" and chatting and laughing with each other at their desks. When the phone rang, any team member would reach for it without hesitation. They were utterly relieved because they were now able to work with people who respected and appreciated them, and it made every part of their job better.

Helping the team contribute in a way that means your firm's marketing draws in the very best clients for you (and sends away the ones you don't want) will have a big impact on their day-to-day job. When I run the Accelerator coaching group, the first session is Audience. It's also chapter one of my book *The Accountant Marketer*, and if you've read that, you'll know that considering your audience is the first question—always—for any marketing action you ever take. It doesn't matter if you use the newest video equipment or build the most amazing-looking website if you haven't considered who it is for. One of the questions I ask in session one of that live coaching group is "Tell me who your favourite client is. Their first name." I tell them not to overthink it: "When I say 'favourite client,' whose name comes to mind? The kind of person you think, *Oh, if only I could have a few (or a hundred) more clients just like them!*" Whenever we do this exercise, the names come thick and fast. Katie. Glen. John. Jamie. Imogen. Varesh. Sian.

You can do this exercise with your team too. Have them write down the first name of their favourite client, and then look at all those favourites together and talk about the qualities those people have. Review other clients and talk about what you love and what's difficult about working with them. Look for patterns together. You could even use this information to create an imaginary client, someone who brings together all the best qualities of the clients you love and appreciate. This involves creativity and, since knowing exactly who you want to work with affects every marketing decision you make, means your team is beginning to be involved in marketing. Best of all, it's easy to do and based on real humans, clients who actually exist, not an imaginary avatar created out of wishes and hopes.

As you think about the qualities your very best clients have, your attention can turn to the values your firm stands for. How might you include creativity within those values? It could be the word "creativity" itself, or it could be one aspect of it, such as problem-solving, curiosity, open-mindedness, or experimentation. Your firm values need to reflect who you are as a firm, but some of these values can be *aspirational*: something you don't fully do yet, but you want to. Identify it as a value to make sure it is given the attention it needs. Values are integrated into your marketing—on your website, in a manifesto, in blog posts, on videos—but they go far deeper than that. They are reflected in the team's behaviour, in the words you use, in the way you approach sales calls and service reviews. If "curiosity" is a value you'd like to see more of in the team, setting it (or a similar word) as a value means you're thinking about it. Talking about it. Holding sessions to explore some of the problems you face and how you might address them. Changing the way you run team meets so everyone has an opportunity to speak, ask a question, or suggest a solution. Taking the time to really understand a problem first before you get to the solution.

One good question to ask the team—or get the team in the habit of asking themselves—begins with these three words: "How might we . . . ?" All three words are important. The word "how" reflects the need to be specific. If you're considering changing your onboarding process, and you ask, "How might we welcome new clients?" The question directs you and the team to think about that how. We could . . . send a welcome box full of gifts. We could . . . drop by their place of business with a gift. We could . . . invite them to an evening get-together held at our offices each month.

The next word, "might," reflects the multiple options. We *might* have a team member phone them in the first day or two to ask if they have everything they need. Or we might not do that. We *might* record a welcome video of the whole team, or we might have each individual team member record a welcome video and send the new client the videos from the team members they'll be working most with. "Might" leaves room for options, for openness.

And finally, "we" represents the fact this is a team effort. We could have a sign at the front door with letters we change to welcome the client who is coming into the office. This might involve one team member finding the right kind of sign, another team member ordering it, and each team member responsible for changing the sign letters on the day of their client's visit. *We*, together, are considering options to make this client's experience better. How—might—we?

Take a team retreat

Taking a retreat with your team can be an excellent opportunity to pause, reflect, and practise these creative exercises together. Randy Crabtree, co-founder of Tri-Merit Specialty Tax, has a team of eighty people who all work remotely. "I've always been a person who wants to get to know the person, not the job title," Randy says. "So on our team calls, once a month, there's space for one of the team to spend twenty minutes just talking about who they are and what they love doing. One time, we learned all about fly-fishing and how you tie a fly. We let people share their outside-of-work passions."

Twice a year, the team gets together in person for more opportunities to get to know each other and share who they are. One year, they did a strengths finder exercise, which involves understanding where people fit in terms of four domains: executing, influencing, relationship building, and strategic thinking. Each person on the team moved to one of the four corners of the room identified by that domain, and they were able to look around and see how the whole team fit together. "Seeing people's strengths in that visual way was such a powerful experience. We realised if everyone was over here in the influencer corner, we'd never get anything done. Or if everyone was building relationships, we wouldn't be taking the time to think strategically." They could see the four groups were pretty balanced, and it helped provide a creative perspective for each of the eighty team members.

My creative agency is also remote. In the early days, we'd gather the team from locations all over the UK a few times a year. We'd come together for a few days, choosing a different city each time. We'd read a book together ahead of time and discuss it, have strategy sessions, review our services, come up with new ideas, and do creativity exercises. During one retreat in London, we invited a business coach to run a training session, and she showed up with an entire suitcase of Lego. Together we built visual representations of how we were working together as a team now, how we wanted to be working together, and what the options were for other ways to structure the team. We built our own little working worlds in Lego and compared them to each other's. Only after we'd done this for a few hours did we bring out the whiteboard and start identifying what we wanted to change.

At that time, we had five or six people, so team retreats were easy to organise and deliver. As the team grew, at one point we had twenty people to bring together from multiple countries. In the year the world came to a halt, that year we didn't travel and didn't hold events and didn't really see anyone outside our own homes, we had to adjust our retreating to make the creative connection with each other. Even considering how to deliver a retreat at a time unlike any we'd ever known required our creative skills. At first, we did online-only retreats, and then as soon as we were able, we adjusted again to hybrid retreats. We'd take two or three days away from day-to-day and client work, hold a few sessions online together, and with the remaining time, the team would get together in person by region. We had always chosen a book to read together as a team, so we continued that practice, and we provided a budget so those in the regional get-togethers could choose a creative activity to do together. Once travel opened up again, we held a full in-person retreat for all regions, and after that we began to alternate each year between hybrid or in-person retreats. We've learned a lot about team retreats, and below are some of the principles we found that help them be effective, creative, and motivating.

Take at least two full days out of your normal client work. Everyone sets an out-of-office message, and no one checks work emails, Slack, or any system which will notify them of client work or issues or questions. If you're going to retreat, actually *retreat.* As a leader, you will need to be the best example of this. Be patient as you work out how you do this, how you communicate it to the team and clients, and figure out what works best for your business. We had several retreats where a newer team member didn't realise the three or four hours first thing in the morning on day one were meant for resting, thinking, reading, walking, or doing a creative activity. They'd check into our team Slack channels and suddenly realise they were doing client work while everyone else was posting pictures of painting or walks by the beach or a museum they were visiting. We changed our onboarding to address this so it was clear what retreating meant—for everyone.

Prepare, prepare, prepare. Whether it's an in-person or hybrid retreat, we found we needed about a month of preparation per team member up to a group of about twenty. We calculated the months using the maximum number of team members who would be physically together. For example, we spent eighteen months preparing for our in-person retreat of eighteen people. For a hybrid retreat, with a maximum of six people in a region, we prepared for six months. You'll need to do all the preparation required for any in-person event, including agendas, travel plans, instructions, boundaries, and budgets.

Prepare your clients. Let clients know this is coming, why you're doing it, and how it will benefit them. Your team is spending time together to think differently, ask good questions, reconsider services and how you deliver them, and ultimately seek to be a better team in serving your clients. The first time we ran a major retreat, we began notifying clients several months before we went away, and the team organised their resourcing so they would complete all client work ahead of time and not be rushed when they returned.

Identify what success looks like. There are good feelings associated with running a retreat. You feel glad you've invested in the team this way. They're more motivated and excited and are talking about ideas. You're glad you did it. But, other than gut feel, how do you know it was a success? The simplest way to determine this is to take measurements before and after. Send a survey to the team each month, something like a team experience survey. Set up and gather your net promoter score (NPS) from the team, like you do with clients. Run the average of the last few months of ratings and then compare those to the months after the retreat. Consider those numbers together with that gut feel, those other indicators you're aware of at the edge of your mind.

Choose a book or a theme to establish a retreat purpose. For years, we'd read a book together as a team. As the team grew, we'd read a different book by division. The designers read a book to help them think differently about design, the content writers read one which addresses words or messaging, and the strategists read one about coaching. A book is one of the easiest ways to choose a theme and a consistency of message between sessions and team members. I tend to choose the book based on a cultural or creative aspect I want our discussions to be centred around. Books we've read together in the past include some of the creative books listed in the reading list I share in section 4 as well as books about marketing, leadership, scaling and growth, and cultural resets. Some of these include:

- For content marketing: *They Ask, You Answer: A Revolutionary Approach to Inbound Sales, Content Marketing, and Today's Digital Consumer* and *The Visual Sale: How to Use Video to Explode Sales, Drive Marketing, and Grow Your Business in a Virtual World* by Marcus Sheridan
- For scaling your marketing: *Oversubscribed: How to Get People Lining Up to Do Business with You* and *24 Assets: Create a Digital, Scalable, Valuable and Fun Business That Will Thrive in a Fast Changing World* by Daniel Priestley
- For scaling your business: *Traction: Get a Grip on Your Business* by Gino Wickman
- For working methods: *Deep Work: Rules for Focused Success in a Distracted World* by Cal Newport
- For working together as a team: *Rising Strong: How the Ability to Reset Transforms the Way We Live, Love, Parent, and Lead* by Brené Brown
- For managers: *Radical Candor: Be a Kick-Ass Boss Without Losing Your Humanity* by Kim Scott

When considering what book is best for the entire team to

read together, consider one with enough variety to cover different roles, divisions, and regions as well as a common thread uniting them all. Some books were right for us a few years ago; others, we wouldn't have been ready for in the early days.

If you choose not to use a book as your theme, you'll need something to bring together the purpose of your retreating. Even something as simple as coffee or podcasting or travel could be your theme if every aspect of the retreat circles back to that theme. You could learn about how coffee is made, go to a coffee roastery together, buy and roast coffee beans, invite a barista to teach you their ways, and make notes about what you've learned or how it applies to delivering a better service.

The team of the accounting firm MAP hold development days every quarter, and part of the day includes a values activity based around the firm's four core values: Be dependable, be caring, be a team player, and be brave. One of the activities for the "be dependable" value involved providing the team with a load of random stuff—wood, bolts, tape, screws, nails, those kinds of things. The team was split into several groups, each of which needed to work together to build something which would drop a ball and roll it across the room. Because of the nature of the exercise, the team had to be creative, says Paul, MAP's owner. "There weren't any rules. They had to come up with their own way, and when they did, the confetti came out, and they knew they'd completed the journey." The MAP team finds this kind of exercise important for reinforcing how they work as a team of accountants. Bookkeeping has to hand over their work to the accountant, who then gives it to the finance partner, who provides it to the client. If any one step fails, they all fail and the client doesn't get what they need.

MAP's development days are a break from the regular accounting work, but "it's not like they're trapped doing that work," Paul said. "They don't want me to jump up every five minutes with a new idea. They want to be productive." Sometimes when a development day is coming up, it's tempting for the team to think, *Oh, there is so much work to do.* But then when the day comes, they're having fun and expressing themselves. They get to do something away from the day job, which is exciting, and it lights them up. And then when the day is done, they go back to the other kind of work they enjoy doing.

Minimise the heavy-duty thinking and working sessions. In the old days of retreats, I thought I needed to cram the days full of sessions. It was a working day, after all! We needed to work—but work creatively, of course! In a hybrid retreat, we'd start with a session for an hour or two, take a break, hold another, have lunch, hold another session, take a break, and have another get together online in the evening. Then we'd do the same again the next day. After the retreat, we talked about what worked and what didn't, what we liked and what wasn't so helpful. Almost every team member shared the retreat was motivating and inspiring and full of ideas . . . and also rather exhausting. Instead of going back into client work refreshed, everyone simply felt like we'd done more work than usual, and now we were all behind. Now our three-day hybrid retreats are more likely to have one major session across all regions on day one, with space for rest and personal creative time. There are regional get-togethers on the second day and another final session on the third day. You can mix it up in whatever way works best for your team and divisions and regions, but don't overdo. Creativity works best when it has some guidelines and space to breathe.

Create a cultural reset

Once you've held creative sessions, considered your values (on your own and together with your team), and taken retreats to stir up creativity and pause and reflect, it may be time for a cultural reset.

Resetting the culture of your business means recognising "what got us here might not get us there." The values, attitudes, and styles of doing business which worked for you ten, five, or even one year ago might not be what moves you into the next phase of your business life. When I decided to find a non-executive director to support me as a business owner, I was ten years into running my business. I thought I had a pretty good idea of what worked and what didn't. And in the early years, I did. When it was only me in the company or when I was working with freelancers and outsourcers or when we hired our first few team members, I was able to figure that out on my own. But as we added team members and managers and built in lines of management and a leadership team, I was faced with the realisation that the culture we had was beginning to form itself into something new, and we needed to recognise it and talk about it.

A cultural reset is needed when the culture has already begun to change—either in a way you appreciate and want to see more of, or in a way you're not sure you want the company to go. If it's positive, it could be that you were intentional about the changes yourself or in leadership but this intentionality has been subtle rather than stated. The reset simply means you take time with the team to address it. Use an existing team meet or a session within a team retreat. Call out the change in culture for what it is, explain why the shift has happened, and how it will help all of you and your clients and the company as a whole. Talk together about what feels uncomfortable or worrying or confusing. Hold sessions with the team to point out the changes, and talk about it together or break out into groups to discuss them. These changes could be things like "We talk about fails together as a team" or "We consider every side of the problem before jumping to solutions." If you've been building creativity into the fabric of your business with these creative exercises, sharing this book with the team, and beginning to reconsider your company values, this is your opportunity to solidify the changes from ideas and experimentation into the way forward.

If you *haven't* made the shifts you want to see, your reset needs to begin earlier. Simply gathering the team together and *telling* them "We're going to do things this way now" will not stir up enthusiasm. It may even result in fear or frustration or doubt this will actually happen. Be honest with yourself as you look at how you've approached things in the past. Has there ever been a time you've decided to make a change and found it hard to get the team on board? Have you or one of the leaders instituted a new way of things, only to see it crumble and everyone go back to the old way?

Years before I set up PF, I worked as a consultant with hundreds of accounting firms across Europe, helping them institute a new way of doing business development (now known as "advisory") in their firm. For many firms used to doing and charging only for compliance work, this meant a complete mindset shift as they began to create services around the advisory work they were doing but not charging for. In principle, they were capable of making this change; in practicality, it didn't always work out. I'd see firms where the team—or even other partners who weren't on board yet—wasn't as enthusiastic about the new way because they didn't come into the firm to deliver business strategy or development services. They liked the old way, the comfortable day-to-day work the firm had been doing for years, sometimes twenty or thirty or even a hundred years. Other firms would create an entire business development division or a new company to deliver these new advisory services. They'd rebrand, build a new website, and send team members to training workshops or business development conferences. But often the cultural change would suffer and struggle and even die out completely because the cultural change flowed from one partner who made the decision on their own and didn't bring along even one other person in the firm, much less the rest of the team.

One firm I worked with saw great success for several years. They doubled their revenue, quadrupled the firm's profits, and had one person running an entire consultancy division to deliver the new services. They ran business owner workshops, and one of the four partners was designated as the full-time Business Development Partner, a newly created role. And yet other than the one person who was managing the consultancy division, everyone else in the firm simply carried on doing things the way they always did them. There were a few team members who entered into the new way with enthusiasm, but they were the exception rather than the rule, and after a year or two, those with the energy and enthusiasm moved on to other places and other roles. After four years, the firm decided to close the consultancy division and go back to the compliance work they were more comfortable with, and the whole team breathed a sigh of relief because that's what they'd wanted all along.

The decision for that firm may have been the best one. Perhaps the new way didn't fit their approach, their culture, and their values. It's also possible they had an amazing opportunity and didn't make it what they could because the new way wasn't supported by a cultural reset. New services were handed to the team, not built by them. New mindset shifts were experienced by the clients, but not the team members. One partner helped build the new division, but none of the other partners wanted to be involved. It was like a stool which needed four legs and only had one. It was bound to crumple at some point, and it did. Ultimately you need to know what problem you're actually trying to solve.

EVERY GOOD MARKETING CAMPAIGN STARTS WITH A PROBLEM TO SOLVE

Marketing isn't about telling people about your company or detailing your services. There are elements of those within your marketing, but its purpose is to help people see a potential solution to a problem they are facing. Whatever they're struggling with—shoes that don't fit, an outdated computer, hiring the wrong team members time after time, getting business funding—marketing says, "There's a way to solve this! And we're here to help." Marketing makes you visible to the people who need you.

I talk about this in chapter 2 of my first book, *The Accountant Marketer*. After you've considered your audience (chapter 1), you then consider the issues they are facing. What is preventing them from reaching happiness, success, or growth?

When you approach marketing this way, building a marketing campaign isn't reduced to a list of actions. Create these website pages, design this guide, run these ads. Instead, the actions you need to take become clear after you've identified who you're talking to and what they're suffering most from. The creative element of problem-solving will help you here.

The kind of advert that asks "Are you wondering what kind of shoes can help your sore back?" is not an example of good marketing. No one is walking around their house or in the woods thinking, *You know, my back is so sore. I wonder what shoes would help?* In their wondering, they're not leaping to the one solution that company happens to provide. What they're really wondering is *Why is my back so sore?* or *What could I try that I haven't tried yet?* Good marketing speaks in a way that fits exactly with these wonderings and helps the potential buyer see a solution they may not have even known existed.

When you bring the two elements of problem-solving and

curiosity to your marketing, it protects you from some of the typical pitfalls accountants experience in marketing.

The first pitfall is to copy what other accountants are doing. Now, let me be clear—borrowing ideas isn't copying. If you get an idea from what someone else is doing and figure out a way to adapt it so it fits your firm and your audience, that's totally okay. Austin Kleon tells us to "steal like an artist" in his book of the same name. He suggests you keep a swipe file, a place where you keep track of things you've borrowed from others. This can be your place of inspiration.

But when you see another accounting firm creating a dance video or setting up a TikTok channel or sending out weekly newsletters, it feels like an easy fix to do almost exactly what they're doing. After all, their videos have hundreds of thousands of views, so they must be doing something right. You found their newsletter intriguing, so it must be working for them. The problem with that approach is you may not be stealing in the artistic sense, taking an idea and getting inspiration from it and making it your own. Instead, you're just stealing. You're taking a marketing action or a format of marketing exactly as it is. Instead of a concept adapted for your audience, your ideal client, and taking into consideration the issues they face, you're taking someone else's idea which came from the needs of their audience. They might have thought, *I wonder if our younger clients would engage more with the team on TikTok videos. Let's try it!* Their marketing actions included setting up the channel and coming up with creative ideas for videos and recording and posting the videos and sharing them to get more views. If you try the same thing, but you don't have the same audience of younger business owners or influencers using social every day, it could completely fail for you. Instead, use your creative skills to understand what problem your audience is facing and how you might share with them a potential solution. Create the kind of content which introduces you as the kind of firm they want to get in touch with.

Creativity Exercise

Pick a company you've visited or bought from in the past month that offered a unique experience you were impressed by. Make notes about this: What did they do? When did it happen? What did you expect, and how did this experience make you feel? Then think about something small you can change or try in your firm based on this experience.

In the second pitfall, you're distracted by the new shiny thing ("*Squirrel!*"). You will always want to drop the project you started for a newer, better, shinier, more attractive idea. The right way in marketing is the long way: consistent, steady creation in the same direction, often for a lot longer than you expected. As with all long ways, there are three stages, and it's always the middle bit which is hardest. It's like the *Two Towers* book in the Lord of the Rings trilogy. I remember the first time I read all three books, starting with *The Fellowship of the Ring*, moving on to *The Two Towers*, and ending with the glorious finish in *The Return of the King*. In the first book, it's all very exciting. The journey is beginning and the fellowship is heading off and you're figuring out who's in and who's not, who's for Frodo and who isn't. In the final book, the journey is coming to a glorious close, and there's a battle, and you're on tenterhooks wondering what will happen and will Frodo make it, and it's all very exciting. But in the middle, in *The Two Towers* . . . it's basically two small hobbits walking for a long time and getting tired. Oddly enough, I remember liking *The Two Towers* the best. There were deep things there. Good conversations and insights. I reread that book more than the others because it had depth and a day-to-day reality I could relate to.

When you've started a new marketing project, it's all exciting and shiny. This is going to be the best website, brand, video series, social media campaign *ever*! When you finish and launch it, you feel proud and receive accolades and see leads trickling in or maybe even flowing in. It's rewarding. But the real work comes in the middle, when you have another video to record, but you've started late because your child was sick in the night and your brain feels like mush. Or your ring light stops working. Or you're working on the video script and, as the content writers at PF put it, "the words aren't wording." At that point, something will appear which looks far more appealing than the project you are currently struggling with, and it will look like a much easier fix. Surely if you put the video series on pause and started doing social ads, *that* would have the impact you're looking for. If you give in to that and start working on the ads, you'll hit your *Two Towers* moment again and be presented with another shiny thing, and the cycle continues endlessly. There's great value in keeping going, which we'll talk about in section 6. Use your creative skills to examine what the problem truly is, whether this is still the right project to solve it and whether there's an adjusted approach you might try which will still help you get to where you want to go. Rather like Frodo and Sam, who were convinced to follow Gollum up the winding stair rather than march through the Black Gates. They still made progress in their journey, but it wasn't quite the way they'd imagined.

The third pitfall is the creation of generic content. Without a creative approach, you'll have bland statements trying to appeal to everybody, which end up appealing to nobody because they're covering so many bases. Generic content has to work too hard, and it doesn't get results. Churning out content for the sake of "doing marketing" looks like saying, "Our modern, forward-thinking accounting assists the small- to medium-sized business entrepreneur to thrive in today's dynamic business landscape by leveraging technology and staying up to date with industry trends." That's a lot of words to say nothing appealing to your ideal audience. No one is thinking, *Oh my word. I'm a small- to medium-sized business entrepreneur! I want to thrive in today's dynamic business landscape!* Instead, reconsider what problem they are really talking and thinking about. How might you share that problem so it fits their personality, their style? The content you create for an audience of gamers will be entirely different from an audience of lawyers. Create the content for the human with their issues, not for yourself.

This leads us to the final pitfall, which is self-focused marketing. When you remember your creative skills, they direct you to the kind of questions (and answers) relating to the kind of people you want to work with. Curiosity means you question everything. What do they care about? What kind of things seem to be typical of accountants and are frustrating to them? How might you address this fear or frustration and ease their concerns? Your marketing then becomes all about them, what they think and wonder and are worried about. That makes it better marketing because marketing is not for you.

Just get started, and just keep going: Consistency in the same direction produces results

There's an image you may have seen, which shows two people digging for diamonds underground, using pickaxes to smash into the dirt. One person gets to a certain point, drops their pickaxe in despair, and goes back to the surface. The image shows how close this person was to the diamonds. Perhaps only one more good smash with the pickaxe and they would have reached their goal and gathered in the treasure. I've sketched out my own version of this image.

It's really hard to know when to stop and when to keep going. I believe in giving up when it's the right thing to do. Continuing something—a project, a business, a relationship—without ever asking questions or considering whether it's the best use of your energy isn't the smartest approach. But most of the time, especially when it comes to marketing, we give up too early. In *The Accountant Marketer,* I mention the average time it takes for true content marketing to deliver that drip feed of results: three years. That can feel discouraging. What else is faster? Where's the shortcut? Do I really have to do good-quality work for that long?

Yet when we look at anything worth having in this life, we know the right way is the long way. This is true for improving our health, building a relationship, and raising children. There are good days and dark days. We hit many points at which we want to throw in the towel (or pickaxe). Often, we *do* drop the pickaxe, crawl out of the tunnel, and sit outside on the grass saying, "I'm never going down there again." But minutes or hours or days later sees us heaving a deep sigh, turning round, and delving into the tunnel again.

I have a mug I use when I'm out for hikes and walks in the Scottish Highlands and on the islands. It has the words "Just keep going" on it in my own handwriting. I have some traditions when I use this mug: I don't drink from it until I've arrived somewhere significant. It's for an achievement, a success in walking. When I set out to climb a hill and climb it. When I intend to reach a waterfall and finally get there and drink water flowing from it. When I reach the halfway point of a day's walk.

It all began years ago with a tin enamel mug I got at an accounting conference. The words on the mug were "Just get started," which I liked and agreed with. We can bemoan where we're at or what we haven't achieved, but sometimes it's merely a matter of picking up the pen or shoes or paintbrush and getting started. I remember well the day I set off on the Isle of Mull for a full day of walking and thought, "Hey, what if I brought a flask of hot coffee and this tin mug with me?" I felt a little foolish for never considering it before, but having the new mug made me think of it. So I did, and I discovered it was a real game-changer to be walking for hours in the cold wind or pouring rain or going sea swimming and being able to stop and enjoy a hot drink in my little mug.

I used that mug for years and loved the reminder that getting to some of the most beautiful places on Earth (or in life) happens when you simply *walk out the door.* Or set off on the drive. The journey of ten miles or a hundred miles or a thousand miles does, indeed, start with one step. Then one day, on one of these walks, I discovered something different. I started off, and I walked, and I got really weary. The views weren't that amazing, and the sky wasn't showing off. Everything was grey, including my mood. I kept walking, one foot in front of the other, almost because the path was there, not because I wanted to keep walking it. I stopped for tea using my "just get started" mug, and then I just . . . kept going. Eventually I found an amazing ravine and waterfalls and views, and the sun came out. I realised getting started is good, and keeping going takes you further.

So I sketched out the words "Just keep going" and spent weeks finding a place to make the mug exactly as I wanted. Not too big, not too small. Comfortable to hold and able to fit easily in a small backpack. The words visible whichever way you hold it (for the pics, obvs). In bright yellow for cheer and creativity and my signature colour. And my familiar "KLR" initials on the bottom because I designed it and I'm proud of it.

Those two always go together. You have to get started, and you have to keep going. That's how you get to the beautiful places or build healthy habits or finish the book. We'll talk more about keeping going at the end of the book. For now, let's turn our attention to when things don't work out along the way: dealing with failure.

SECTION THREE:

Why you resist it

3 WHY YOU RESIST IT

GOOD CREATIVITY INCORPORATES FAILURE

All this talk about creativity can get you thinking about the positive side of it all. New opportunities, motivation, wins. There's also the other side of creativity, which involves failure.

Fails happen, and they contribute to a better result in the long run. I was going to say fails are okay, but they're actually not. It's not a good thing when you make a mistake and the client ends their relationship with you. Or when you hire someone who isn't right for your firm and they cost you weeks, months, even years of lost time. But fails do happen. And on the positive side, they always lead to a learning, or rather they can lead to a learning when we approach them creatively.

Learning by failure is something you as an accountant seek to avoid. Part of this has to do with the nature of accounting: You're looking for the right answer, the correct way to account for these numbers. Making sure the books balance. We're told what the right way is, we do it, and, yes, we'll fail now and then along the way, but every system and process you create is there to prevent the failure. It doesn't feel normal to *expect* to use fails to learn. Personally, it's also less enjoyable. We'd rather learn from other people's mistakes or read books or take courses or figure out how to catch ourselves before the fail happens. Unfortunately, the single best way to have something seared into your memory is through a fail and it pushes you to think creatively. What went wrong? In this chapter, you'll consider how to question everything and ask yourself what you learned and what system needs to change. For now, begin to consider the impact of a fail as a means of creative movement for yourself and for your team.

> *I used to filter any new idea with questioning or second-guessing. I would put myself in the shoes of what I was "supposed" to do. I felt I was breaking the rules if I did something true to me—"Oh, you can't do that. You're supposed to do this. That's what everybody else does." And yet in service of being like everyone else, I felt like I lost myself. I only got it back through being true to myself and seeing the positive reinforcement and ecstatic reactions people had to me being* me *again.*
>
> —*Scotty Scarano, founder of* Accounting High *podcast*

Scotty Scarano told me about the time he decided their firm would do advisory for all their clients. He signed up himself and his whole team for a week-long bootcamp. "I spent over $20,000 on training and teaching everyone to do advisory for the better part of a year," Scotty remembers. "I thought we were going to make millions. Double our fees for all our clients. Everything was awesome!" And yet when it came to finally releasing this new way of doing things to their clients, it was an absolute fail. "Everybody almost quit," Scotty said. When it came to the team doing it on their own, it turned out clients weren't reacting and weren't signing up because the team wasn't excited about it. They'd meet with clients and do the demo and share the pitch, but ultimately, they just wanted to be an accountant and do the accounting work. "I realised I was only really excited about the money," Scott reflected. "It was only when I was okay with letting go of that when we were able to let the whole thing go." He saw everything else in the firm was working and profitable, but this wasn't, and it was time to call it. "That felt like a fail—and it still kind of does. I kept trying to push it, insisting it would work, that everyone would be better. But they didn't care about making more money. They just wanted to do their thing."

Three years later, as Scotty reflected on the experience, he says, "It wasn't a full failure. It wasn't until very recently, last week, I realised how impactful that training was in many other ways. The skills it provided to the team, the ideas it stirred up, affected us more than I realised at the time. Now we are looking at putting together our own solution, and that experience, that 'failure,' is part of that."

> *If it wins, celebrate it. If it fails, sunshine it.*
>
> —*Reed Hastings and Erin Meyer,* No Rules Rules: Netflix and the Culture of Reinvention

Within my own agency, we have a channel called "Fails and learnings" where team members can post something that didn't work or they got wrong or got mixed up. We want space where we can be open about things that didn't work or aren't working and help everyone to learn from them. We created this channel after reading the book *No Rules Rules* about the culture at Netflix and how it helps their team be more creative. One of their cultural guidelines recognises that failing happens. If it's a win, they celebrate it. And if it's a failure, they don't make a big deal about it. They "shine a light on every failed bet" so they can learn from it. When we read this as a team, we felt resistance to it at first. "We don't want to focus on failing," we said. "We're more positive than that." We created a channel for the team to post in, but we only called it "Learnings" because we didn't want to even say the word "fail." Since then, we've renamed it "Fails and learnings" because we're still learning that accepting failure as an expected part of creativity helps us lean into that creativity better.

The more open our culture is, the more each team member can be enthusiastic about building their skills and eager to discuss how they individually, and we as a team, can serve our clients best. When we deliver a draft of a design we're creating and the accountant says, "It's not really what I wanted," a creative mindset allows us to receive that positively and work more efficiently to solve the underlying problem. As we talk with the accountant, they may be reminded marketing isn't about their own personal preferences but rather their audience's preferences, and they might discover that what has been created is really appealing to the kind of clients they want more of. So actually it's spot on, and we can continue with the project. Or as we explore what happened and what doesn't feel like a fit, our team might realise we missed something in the early stages. Perhaps we didn't dig deep enough into the audience, and we were missing clarity about who exactly this is for and how it will appeal to them. Fixing that is a win for everybody. For us, it's a learning about our design process; for the accountant, a learning about who marketing is for; and for the accountant's prospective client, an appealing design which helps them recognise they want to work with this accountant.

Creativity Exercise

Pick a fail you or your firm has experienced in the past month, something you tried that went either slightly or spectacularly wrong. What is the number one learning you got from that? If you haven't already, share that with your team.

Failure is something we as accountants tend to resist, but the more we embrace failure as part of creativity, the better we are able to deliver our very best work. Let's look at the story of the shitty pots.

Quantity over quality leads you to quality: The story of the shitty pots

David Bayles and Ted Orland, in their book *Art and Fear: Observations On the Perils (and Rewards) of Artmaking*, tell the story of a ceramics teacher who split his class into two groups. One would focus on quality, making the very best ceramic pot and only one; the other would focus on quantity, making as many ceramic pots as they possibly could. The results would be graded accordingly. In the quality group, they'd need a near-perfect pot to get the highest grade. In the quantity group, their work would be literally weighed on scales, and the more pots, the higher the grade.

When grading time came, "A curious fact emerged," the authors say. "The works of highest quality were all produced by the group being graded for quantity. It seems that while the 'quantity' group was busily churning out piles of work—and learning from their mistakes—the 'quality' group had sat theorizing about perfection, and in the end had little more to show for their efforts than grandiose theories and a pile of dead clay."

We'd expect the quality group to win out. They had all that time and only one pot to make! Piece of cake, right? The problem is that in order to get to our wins, our perfect pot, we've got to fail and learn from it along the way. We have to make a lot of shitty pots if we're going to craft the perfect one.

Yes, the quantity group churned out shitty pot after shitty pot, especially at the beginning, but they learned on the job. They literally felt what it was like to do something which resulted in cracks or lumps or a flat pancake instead of a pot. Conceptual learning doesn't help you create better. And it might even fool you into thinking you are creating the most perfect pot (or blog post or video or website page) when, in fact, it's only adequate. You haven't written enough shitty blogs or recorded enough shitty videos or published website pages which didn't work.

Make your shitty pots. If you want to get better at writing, write more. Write social posts and blog posts and email content and copy for a PDF guide. Write book chapters. The more you write, the better you will get, even if a lot of that writing doesn't seem very good at the time. Maybe it isn't very good. But that's not the point. You're using the quantity approach to learn.

This works exceptionally well for videos too. I remember one Friday when I had four videos I needed to record. Not short unscripted ones for a team member or a client but the ones we use in our sales process and on our website. They needed a script, a purpose, intentionality, and energy. There were time limitations. I don't usually plan to record that many videos at one go; I find it takes a great deal of energy, and it can take far longer than I expect. But a few things had cropped up, including travel and sickness and a few business surprises (you know the way), so I was down to the wire.

Oh, and three of the videos were a re-record; our marketing director had reviewed some I'd created earlier and pointed out issues which made the videos less effective. So I not only needed to record a lot of videos, but I had to redo ones I'd considered done. I woke up that morning in a very grumpy mood. I did not want to record those videos. I wasn't feeling it. I definitely wasn't motivated. But the deadline loomed before me, and I decided to do everything within my power to make the best videos I was capable of in spite of my mood. So I started with an internal one for the team that required the most energy, the most creativity. I played music. I sketched out little notes on paper and held them up. I chair danced.

And my motivation lifted a bit. Hey, look at what I was able to create! If I can do that on my worst day, what could I be capable of if I kept going? So I kept going. On to the next videos, the three re-records.

They were still hard. I stopped and started a lot. After a few hours of eye-rolls, blank pauses, lots of swearing, and significant edits, I had three more videos done. I won't say they were the best videos I've done, but they were done, and they were definitely an improvement over the previous versions. Then an amazing thing happened. Because of all the stops and starts, the repetition of recording and editing had gotten smoother. I'd gotten into a flow. I found myself thinking, *Are there any other videos I still need to record?* I dived into my list and found a few others outstanding, so I recorded those too. I recorded a few short reels to use on our Instagram feed another day. I was in the zone. I ended up recording seven videos that day—and not just recording them but editing and publishing, uploading and sharing them. The concept of the shitty pots had come through again.

What is it you want to get really good at creating? How can you apply the quantity principle to it? Here are some examples.

Video: Record a sixty- or ninety-second Instagram reel every day for a month. Play with the editing, the music, the captions, the GIFs. See what's possible. Produce some really shitty videos. By the end of the month, I guarantee your most recent video will be better than your first one.

Writing: Give yourself a word count and start your day by reaching that word count before you open email, before you get lost in all the weeds of the day. It could be something as simple as two hundred words a day. It doesn't even have to be good writing. It can be gobbledygook. But put your hands to the keyboard, write until you've hit your word count, and then stop.

Social media: Create a social post every day for a month. You could put these posts on one platform, or split it up and do three posts on Instagram and four on LinkedIn. These don't have to be long or groundbreaking or "professional." Use what's in front of you that day. Did you have a great meeting with a client? Talk about that. Did you go to the beach with the kids and the dog? Share a photo or a short video of the waves.

Creativity Exercise

Pick video, writing, or social media. In that category, create something every day for a month—a short video, a total word count, a social post. At the end of the thirty days, look back and identify one thing you've learned which you can use in your firm's marketing.

Beyond marketing, you could apply this to other areas of your business. You could improve your onboarding by creating a Google doc and every day adding content for one email in your onboarding process. Work on your company values by documenting one thing after every team meet and every client meeting that relates to what you stand for, what you don't, and what matters to you and your firm. Change your sales process by editing a small part of your proposal template every day, over and over, sometimes making it better and sometimes making it worse. It will sort itself out. Your quantity approach will deliver in the end.

As accountants, you find the quality approach appealing because it feels like it will mean fewer fails. You can sit quietly in your office for months, building the perfect onboarding system, and when it's ready, you sweep aside the curtains and reveal what you have created. Ta-daaa! You have crafted the greatest onboarding process known to humanity and to the accounting industry at large, and the world will—oh. Whoops. That first email you wrote two months ago isn't quite relevant anymore because you changed a few things since then. Okay, fix that, sweep aside the curtain, ta-daaa! It's here, it's perfect, it's—oh. Actually, there are two new team members now whose names need to be added to the team list . . . and so it goes.

One of the ways I coach accountants through the Accountant Marketer principles is in a series of twelve intensive sessions. Working one-to-one on a weekly basis, we study these principles as they apply to this accountant, this firm. Each week, the accountant identifies some new idea or content piece, and that becomes their homework before the next session. One intensive member, Zach, expressed at the beginning of the sessions there was so much content and messaging which needed to change for his firm, but it all felt a bit overwhelming. Where would he even start? After all, he wasn't a content writer or a designer. As we worked through the principles in order, starting with considering his audience and their issues, his firm's process and way, their values and philosophy, he started thinking about the things he kept repeating to potential clients. I could almost see the gears in his mind turning. By the next week, he'd created a rough sketch, showing "Our Team," "Our Work," "Our Tech," "Our Clients," and how all these worked together. By the following week, after a few more prospect calls, he started to see how he could simplify it. So he adjusted the sketch to include three categories of "Our Work," "Our Journey," and "What Defines Us." The graphic continued to go through additional iterations, but it all came from his head. And over a period of twelve weeks, he simply adjusted it slightly every week based on the kinds of real-life conversations he was having with prospective clients until it summarised what his buyers needed to know.

It truly works best when you start with the bare bones of a system and add to it every day. With every new client, every new prospect, you make a tweak or a change. That's the quantity approach. It's faster, it's more realistic, and it reflects a changing business. Yes, it includes a few fails along the way, but the end result is a much better system. Or blog post. Or video. Or ceramic pot.

PERMISSION TO FAIL

As accountants, you want to get the *right* answer. You figure with enough checklists and rules, you can do that yourself, and you can help your entire team do it too. The problem with applying this kind of thinking to the creative mindset is that you're trying to teach others how to create the one perfect pot based on all the shitty pots you created. This doesn't work. They've got to create their own shitty pots too. That means accepting fails for yourself, your team, and your business as it grows. Yes, the balance needs to be there; we don't seek out failure, and we don't brush it off like it doesn't matter. But we also don't seek to build systems which avoid failure because then you avoid the heart of creativity.

Accepting failure and its related learnings is part of creativity, not because we like or enjoy failure (we don't) but because we don't hold onto failure as a reflection of our identity. A fail doesn't mean you personally are a failure. It doesn't mean you have no idea how to run your firm or that everything is a disaster. What it means is that you are human. What matters more than the failure is the way you respond when the conversation was difficult, or the client left, or got angry at you. When the applicant or team member didn't work out. When you screwed up, when it broke, when you missed the deadline. When someone complains or is upset or doesn't understand.

When this happens, there are two questions for you to ask.

The first is "What will I learn?" And the second is "What system needs to change?" Those two questions protect you from being defensive, laying blame, or, worst of all, ignoring what happened and seeing it happen again and again in the future.

What will I learn, and what system needs to change?

With any fail, there is always something to learn about yourself. Ask yourself questions like:

- How did I respond? What does that tell me?
- How do I feel? Where does that come from?
- Did I have any gut feelings about this? Why did I take action, or why didn't I?
- What do I tend to do, feel, think, and act when these kinds of things happen? Is that how I want to respond in future?

There will also be something you can learn about the thing—the client, the product, the software, the hiring process. You can learn what works and what doesn't. What you enjoy and what you don't. You can ask:

- Is this something I enjoy? Do I like working with this type of client?
- Do I need more training or help with this thing?
- How does it actually work?
- Who else is doing it well?

Asking about what system needs to change will help protect you from making the mistake again. Ask questions like:

- How did this happen in the first place? What led to this happening?
- What is our system now? Do we have one at all?
- If we don't have a system, what would a basic one look like?
- If we have a system, what broke or didn't happen or didn't work as we expected? What did we miss, if anything? What did we let slide?
- What one small thing could I change right now to begin to improve this system?

Answering that last question will deliver the greatest impact over time. It's tempting to think you need to block out an entire day (at least) to build the right system. Plan it out with maps and whiteboards and wireframes. Hire a consultant. Prepare a change management strategy. In actuality, the best systems aren't created in a day. In the same way Zach's cornerstone graphic improved slightly every week as he spoke to potential clients, the best systems are built when you 1) just get started and 2) slightly adapt what you have with every real-life situation that impacts your system.

Sales and onboarding are the two systems which show this principle in the most obvious way. You could work for days or months on building the perfect sales system, only to discover in the next sales call that you missed something significant. Perhaps you focused the entire sales process on what you and the team do, how much it costs, and when it starts, and the prospect wants to know what they're expected to do and when the payments happen. Those things are helpful and need to be folded into your sales system, but they were revealed more clearly when the prospect asked about them.

The same applies for onboarding. You and the team could craft the most amazing onboarding ever known to an accounting firm (cue angels singing), only to onboard your next client and have them ask a question about the one thing you forgot to include. Maybe you were so focused on building the payment system that you didn't include the link. Or you did include a payment link, but your new client is from another country with different tax requirements, and you now need to provide two links.

When creating your system, *presume* you're going to miss something. Be okay with it. Recognise it is coming, and it will help make your system better. The thing you didn't account for—that thing that feels like failure—is your next step towards that amazing system which *will* work brilliantly once it's based on real life and real clients. This could look as simple as opening up a document and writing out in numbered format what happens the moment a prospect enquires about working with you. For every item you write down, ask a question about it.

1. Number one, the form comes in from the website. What other ways might someone get in touch about working with you? How will you include that in your system?
2. Number two, you reply to the form by email. Who does this when you are away or on holiday? Do you have a template for how you reply? Do you include a link to book a meeting, or do you call them?
3. Number three, they book a meeting. What happens if they never book the meeting? What if the meeting is booked and needs to change? Who might they book the meeting with besides you?
4. Number four, you hold the meeting. Is there an agenda? Do they fill in a questionnaire beforehand? What happens if they don't fill it in? How long is the meeting?
5. Number five, you prepare a proposal . . .

. . . and so on.

Every step leads you to document another step. And every real-life scenario in which someone fills in a form (or doesn't) or shows up for a meeting (or brings four people into the meeting) provides you with one more small update to make your system move more smoothly and reflect the way sales meetings really go, not the way you imagine they go in your mind.

Reframe your thinking

The great news about failing is that most of the fails you'll experience in marketing won't have nearly the level of consequences you might imagine at first. You may have heard of big marketing fails by companies like Coca-Cola, when they decided to change the recipe of Coke and came out with New Coke. It was a complete disaster, and they had to go back to the original recipe. There's an anecdotal story (still unconfirmed) about when Pepsi used the tagline "the new generation," which, translated into another language, meant something similar to "it brings your ancestors back from the dead." It's true—these kinds of marketing disasters can have a huge impact on big companies. But you're not Coke or Disney or Google; you're a small- to medium-sized accountancy firm, and in my experience, the biggest marketing mistakes you could make will be the kind which simply don't get very many results and you have to start again. They're not PR blunders; they're just things which don't work out. More likely, your marketing mistakes will impact you more in terms of guilt or fear rather than actual impact.

> *Guilt is arrogant. It means you've taken sides and know you are right.*
> —*Matthew McConaughey,* Greenlights

When you have a marketing fail, or when nothing is

happening at all and that feels like a failure, you're likely to say something like one of these statements:

"I should have started marketing earlier."

"I don't think I did the right things."

"I don't even know where to start."

"This other business did this and that, and I can't be like them."

"It's my fault we're not further than we are."

You might feel like you're being really humble and honest, but it's also possible you're tapping into the arrogance of guilt, taking sides and being sure it's all your fault. Taking responsibility *is* an important factor when you're looking back at what you haven't done. It's good to say "I *could* have done this" or "I'm not sure why I didn't" or "I'd like to do better." But those are all positive and encouraging approaches, whereas guilt lives simply to make you feel worse about something you can't change.

The truth is, you may not ever know for sure if you did the right things or the wrong things. Started too late, started too early, chose the wrong niche, didn't stick at the niche long enough, copied others . . . you don't know. It's good and healthy to ask questions, but I encourage you to simply . . . ask the questions. Without the guilt, without the blame. Just ask.

What *did* I do? When? Why did I do it? What was helpful? Where am I confused? I wonder where that came from? What did I expect to get from that spend? Where did those expectations come from? What are my expectations now?

No matter what the answer, be willing to take the time to sit with it. Don't pile all the blame on because marketing isn't about right or wrong. It's about asking whether you understand. And once you understand, take another action.

Creativity Exercise

Choose a failure you've been feeling annoyed or even guilty about. Ask yourself these three questions: What went well? What went wrong? And what will I do differently? This simple approach can help focus you on the learning, not the guilt.

Not perfect but done: Get it out there

Not everything is a complete fail. Sometimes it's simply imperfect. Getting hung up on perfection will definitely prevent you from achieving more creativity in your marketing and in your life. The good will most definitely become the enemy of the great. As an accountant, you may have the search for perfection in your lifeblood. It gives you strength and energy. We've recognised already why this makes sense for accounting work and why it doesn't make as much sense for creative work. Releasing the mental demand for perfection will make it far more possible for you to get your creative work out there so it can actually help people. After all, most of your creativity is being channelled into what will truly help people: your new onboarding process, a new approach to sales, your book, your podcast. It may feel terrifying to put something out there that isn't perfect, but it's helping literally *no one* if it's sitting forever only in your mind.

Releasing the mental demand for perfection will make it far more possible for you to get your creative work out there so it can actually help people.

Yes, it feels safer there. It may even feel perfect, in a way. No one is reviewing it or commenting or pointing out flaws. No one knows you haven't got your shit together in every single aspect of your business and life. Right now, you've got an illusion of perfection, and releasing your idea or your new action will absolutely shatter that illusion.

Time to break some illusionary glass. Most of you are not celebrities with millions of followers. It makes sense for a world-famous author to hold their drafts close and have people sign nondisclosure agreements and protect their work before the hordes can flood in and criticise it before it's ready. But in the early days, you're talking a few hundred people who are going to see this and comment and absorb and give feedback. Maybe a few thousand at most. Getting your imperfect thing out there—and seen—will help make it a hell of a lot closer to perfect than if it continues to sit quietly in the darkness where no one sees it. Ultimately, you want this thing to be *done*. It's not perfect, but it's out there. The form is there for people to fill in. The video is uploaded and ready to watch. The automation sequence is connected to the email sign-up. You're still doing good work; at the same time, you're accepting that something will absolutely not work. Part of getting it out there is to figure out what that thing is. Get results so you can make adjustments based on those results.

The "not perfect but done" cry can be a difficult one to rally round, not only for accountants but for any business owner or anyone who cares about what they're sharing. After all, it's a reflection on you. The perfect website doesn't exist, but we have reputations to uphold. We want our work to give a good impression and help the buyer understand our expertise without distraction. To look at this from another angle, we can seek for our work to be "not perfect but good."

This means you accept that absolute perfection is impossible, but this marketing item, this project you've worked on, is *good*. There's one clear message appealing to the people this has been created for. It's on-brand and gives a good impression, and it's clear what they do next. You don't panic if there's a small spelling mistake or if one of the images could be better. With most things, you can fix it quickly. Edit the website page and republish. Update the PDF guide and replace it on the same URL. Even if it's a social media post, you can own up to your mistake and share the updated version.

To get to "good" status, consider what you've created and are about to share. First, check it works the way it's intended to. Can they fill in the form, does the page load, is the PDF downloadable, is the video the right length for the platform? Second, make sure it's on-brand. Are the colours right, and does it portray you well? Look at your message. Have you been clear? If there's an action for them to take, is it specific and easy to follow? And finally, consider whether it resonates with the intended audience. Do your clients like it? Does the intended reader or viewer find the topic intriguing? Does it relate to what they're going through on a day-to-day basis?

You can still get amazing results from something imperfect as long as it's still good. And the most important aspect of good is whether you've hit on a message they can connect with. Think of a comedian who says, "Have you ever done this . . . ?" and everyone laughs, and you realise, *Hey, it isn't just me! There are other people—a lot of other people—who feel this way!* I talked with a bookkeeper who told me she had lost count of the number of business owners, particularly female business owners, who asked her, "How do I know if my bookkeeper is doing a good job or not? What am I meant to look for, and what are they meant to be doing?" Because she got this question often, she created content about it. She didn't have to create a ten-video training course or create a new brand for it; she simply wrote out the answers she'd been giving over and over, and this content resonated with the kind of person she often did business with. A simple document or screenshare video or even a sketch with pen and paper can be far more helpful than your perfectly planned, perfectly executed community membership no one joins.

Create the minimum viable product (MVP). This could be the minimum viable blog post, video, training course, guide, or even book. Keep it simple. We love to use tech because it helps us avoid the real question of whether this is useful and if people resonate with it. We can play for hours or days with the buttons and the hex codes. We *feel* like we're making so much progress because we're *busy*. But if you haven't stopped to check proof of concept (does anyone actually want this?) and to consider the worst possible outcomes (as well as the best ones), you could spend twelve months on something no one wants or needs.

No doubt you've seen this before with marketing advertisements for a big or well-known company. A billboard goes up or a new design comes out for a product, and instantly you see what everyone else sees: There's an awkward innuendo or the clever concept doesn't translate well onto a box or a bottle. When this happens, you and most of the rest of humanity are wondering, "How in *the world* did they miss this?" You imagine these suited executives sitting round a boardroom table, coming up with their clever line, nodding and smiling and shaking hands all round. Maybe popping some champagne, saying, "This is going to be the best marketing campaign anyone has ever created!" You wonder why they didn't run it past literally any human in their life, a normal, non-suited executive human, maybe, or perhaps (shockingly) the kind of person who would reach for the bottle when shopping. Or, in this case, grimace and walk away.

This is part of building your MVP: Keep it simple, and check with the real humans who would be using it or reading it or listening. Check with them in a way which makes it easy for them to say, "Um . . . I'm not sure if you've noticed but . . . there's an app that does that already." One of my favourite scenes from the film *The Internship* is when a group of Google interns are trying to come up with a new app idea. The group is made up of mostly young developers plus two older interns, middle-aged guys who know little to nothing about tech. The app ideas the older interns come up with are hilarious because all of us watching the film know *the app already exists*. Of course, they double down and insist theirs is very different because it allows people to take a photograph and share it "on the line," and it's a billion-dollar idea . . . and the young developers are shaking their heads. Yes, it is a billion-dollar idea. It's one which was already created and sold, and people use it every day.

This doesn't mean your creativity is limited or prevented by what's already out there. There are so many books on creativity already; this one you're reading is hardly ground-breaking information. But I've applied this particular topic to a specific audience: you, the accountant. Having a brilliant idea is great; now think about how you are truly making it yours. You're not stealing someone else's idea; you're using what's there as a jumping-off point to create something with a slightly different spin. After all, there may not *actually* be anything new under the sun. Just the same sun with a different perspective. While there are millions of books and podcasts and paintings and blog posts and products, there is only one *you* in the entire universe, from the beginning of time until now. So your voice and perspective matter.

Let's take a step back and look at the broader picture of creativity.

CREATIVITY DOES NOT EQUAL ART

I grew up thinking creativity was art. Painting. Drawing. Photography. Illustrations. Something which stood alone, disconnected from science or logic or facts. Creativity was art, and hard facts were science. But there was an odd disconnect because even as I studied accountancy and got my accounting qualification and worked as an auditor, I was also fascinated by photography. I painted. I drew. I journaled. People told me I was too organised to be creative and too creative to be an accountant.

I knew these two qualities made a strange combination, but I kept exercising them both. My parents encouraged me to get a degree in something practical, something that would be helpful no matter what I chose to do with my life. It was wise advice. I'm grateful for it. I didn't think at the time I would end up working as an accountant, but I found in my university classes that the only ones which truly challenged me were the accounting classes. I wanted to figure out how it worked. I graduated, I got my CPA certification in the States, and I took a job as an auditor.

When I first moved to Scotland, the creative side began working in tandem with the accounting side. I worked in business development for an accounting firm, set up a new consulting division, and then worked with a consulting network for accounting firms. At the same time, I set up a wedding photography business. I enjoyed taking and editing photographs and designing wedding albums. When I set up a creative agency to work exclusively with accountants, I kept shooting weddings and ran both businesses at the same time.

As always happens when you try to give your very best to two different things, I got worn out. I remember my dad saying to me, "You can't go on at this pace. At some point, you'll have to pick one." I remember telling him, "Dad, I can't pick one. I need this creative side. And I'm challenged by this accounting side. If I let go of the photography, I won't have any creative outlet. If I let go of the marketing agency, the opportunities for profitability are harder." Dad was wise and didn't press it, but the seed had been planted.

Because I did wear myself out. I had a breakdown—physically, mentally, emotionally. I was in Tuscany, Italy, part of a retreat delivered by a luxury wedding photographer who had carved a niche photographing weddings at wineries. I had saved for years to experience this workshop and build my skills. I wanted to consider what it really meant to be a photographer, and I wanted to enjoy the beauty and the rest. Only a day or so into the week, I found myself lying on the cold tiles of an Italian bathroom floor, very sick and miserable and wanting to go home. I had pushed myself and pushed myself and was trying to do everything well, and my body was protesting. And I realised Dad was right: I would definitely have to choose.

I looked ahead to the next ten or twenty years and realised the option of building a marketing agency with a team of people, serving clients all over the globe, was far more scalable than this—working constantly to get one-off weddings, spending hours of prep time, carrying around a heavy bag from 7 a.m. to midnight on the day, enjoying the work itself but finding myself utterly exhausted at the end of every one.

So I chose the agency. I stopped taking new weddings, finished the ones I had committed to, and began to feel a little space and freedom opening up in my mind. And to my surprise, I discovered that although I'd cut off the creative flow going into photography, I hadn't cut off creativity entirely. It was still there, but it was simply popping up elsewhere. I started sketching. I wrote more. I took photographs and shot video on my phone. I realised it was still possible for me to have both the creative side as well as the business side.

You can too. The more I've worked with accountants in my

creative agency, the more it has become clear to me that you also hold these two qualities together. It might not be in as dramatic or obvious a way as I did with the marketing and photography businesses, but you have the logic and rules side, and you have the problem-solving and curiosity side.

> *Historically, creativity has always said it's one or the other: You're either science-led or arts-led, and obviously "arts" represents more creativity. I juggled with that for a long time. I think they can co-exist, and should co-exist, and that's really the reason I set up my accounting firm, to be creative around my business but provide an analytical service.*
>
> *—Lauren Harvey, Full Stop Accounts*

Mike Rohde, the author of *The Sketchnote Workbook*, addresses this dichotomy. The practice of sketchnoting allows you to take notes in illustrative form. Rather than obsessively writing down every word the speaker says, you listen for core concepts and take time to think about them as you sketch ideas. If a speaker says, "Would you have a beer with this new client?" it takes longer to sketch out a pint glass than to write out those few words. When I've shared my sketchnotes at accounting conferences, invariably I get responses from accountants saying, "Wow—these are great! I wish I could do it, but I can't draw" or "These are amazing! Too bad I'm not artistic."

Sketchnoting, Rhode says, is about ideas, not art. It doesn't matter if you're artistic (or think you aren't). You don't have to be a painter or an illustrator to try sketchnoting; anyone can sketch out a flower or a tree or a strawberry. You might not think it looks good. You might feel embarrassed about your version of a tree. But where does this come from? Small children aren't embarrassed about their drawings, and sometimes as adults, we need to tactfully say, "Oh wow! Tell me about it!" because we are racking our brains to figure out if this is a tree, a dinosaur, a cookie, or the Empire State Building. (Turns out it was a drawing of you. Obviously.)

The point is, creativity doesn't start by focusing on *getting a result.*

Creativity doesn't start by focusing on *getting a result.*

That's not at the heart of why we create. Yes, there are artists who paint in order to have paintings to sell. Or authors who write books to sell. But most of the time, we create things because we have to. Artists are a good example of this; we now know the stories of artists who were underappreciated in their lifetime, but they kept going because they had to. Because it was simmering inside them, and it needed to come out.

The artists and writers know, too, that it doesn't come out like magic, so they build habits in order to get to a result. Every successful writer I've heard of says the best way to get results in writing is to *write.*

> *Amateurs sit and wait for inspiration, the rest of us just get up and go to work.*
>
> —*Stephen King*

Austin Kleon tells the story of his four-year-old who covered page after page of drawings, spread out in glorious disarray all over the living room floor. He points out his son is not creating these drawings to sell on Instagram or to become a famous artist. After he was done with his prolific drawings, he got up and walked away and did something else. He'd created; that was all he had set out to do, and now he was moving on. We see this childlike approach to creativity in artists who were not appreciated in their lifetime. I remember going to a Monet exhibition at the Phoenix Art Museum, and the quote from one of the painter's journals which stood out to me was this: "I am very depressed and deeply disgusted with painting. It is really a continual torture."

I stared at this quote thinking, *This is reality*. This is how it can feel to create sometimes. You do it, and you keep doing it, and some days you wonder why you're doing it. You may throw down your notebook or close your spreadsheet out of frustration, but you'll pick it back up again. As business owners, as entrepreneurs, we do that too. We have days where nothing seems to be working, and a client is unhappy, and a team member we hired didn't work out, and the brand-new service we were so excited about isn't getting the take-up we expected. It's okay to put down the laptop, to rant or rage or cry if we need to. Sometimes it doesn't work out. But we still get back to it an hour later or the next day, partly because we have to and partly because we want to. There's a motivating challenge in there to figure it out; it's a problem which needs to be solved. There are questions to be asked and curiosity to explore. Our creativity won't let us leave it alone.

All of this is why the connection between creativity and marketing can feel uncomfortable for you. Isn't the point to get results? Aren't you doing marketing to get more leads, grow your business, make life easier for yourself and your team? It's good to set goals for your business and your marketing. You do it with your clients; you need to understand why they're running the business or what matters most to them so you can help them interpret and use their numbers. But if your approach to marketing is solely about your goals, money, and results and doesn't allow for simply creating for its own sake, you miss out on the very best kind of marketing. You miss out on so much potential within yourself. And there's good news for you as an accountant: Creativity may at times flow out in artistic expression, but creativity itself doesn't have to be art.

Creativity Exercise

Pick an animal you like (mine would be a puffin). Set a timer for five minutes. Using either pen and paper or a tablet, sketch as many versions of this animal as you can until the timer goes off. Use your phone to give you ideas to sketch from or copy. Then . . . do nothing with the results. Don't post or share them; just consider what you noticed about the process and the result.

I ran a sketchnoting workshop at the UK Xero headquarters for account managers who helped accountants. When I was preparing, I figured everyone who came to the workshop would know they were creative. After all, Xero uses the words "beautiful" and "human" in all their marketing. The phrase "beautiful accounting software" is trademarked. I figured no one would feel unworthy to be there or worry about how their efforts could look. But still, they did feel that way. I saw people sketching things out and heard them say, "This isn't very good" or "I don't know how to draw" or saying to someone else "Yours is better."

To combat this, we talked about "ideas, not art." We identified the principles behind sketchnoting, and I ran different exercises such as having everyone draw out their own name with some visual representations of themselves—even just shapes. I encouraged them to use their phone to search for images or icons that represented certain topics and copy those. They began to be amazed at what came out of their own pens onto the paper. "Hey—this is actually not too bad!" they said, laughing. We agreed together it wasn't about creating a good drawing but about getting a point across. An idea, not art.

There's still a deep insecurity within accountants about your ability to do what is creative. To come up with good marketing ideas. To write. To shoot video. To take photographs. To be involved in your website design and build. To deliver a really good event. It's not only that you've been told you're not creative; it's that you've said it to yourself. Over and over. Repeating that you can't do it, this isn't in you, it's not your skill. What would happen if you stopped telling yourself that and started looking for the creativity that is actually there? What if you accepted it as fact that you're creative? What would happen next? What would you do with all those ideas that come to you when you're travelling, when talking to a client, when listening to a speaker at a conference?

Some fears might come up. Let's look at those for a moment.

Creativity taps into the childlike wonder and also the adult fears

When you tap into the creativity within you, there's a childlike "you" brought out . . . and sometimes fears and resistances come along with them. True creativity is doing what you want to do simply because you want to do it. The drawing you sketch out on paper or your tablet which nobody sees. The game you make up with your kids when they're bored. The song lyrics you invent at Christmas for a laugh. That's the kind of creativity kids have, and that childlike voice is within all of us, but there's another voice too. It's the one that says, "Everyone is looking at me, so I'd better stop." We've got both voices within us: the one who does fun and hilarious things for the sheer joy of doing it and the one who holds back and says, "Someone will see! Someone will laugh! Someone will . . ."

You often see it in the transition from child to teenager. I was on a beach with a twelve-year-old, and we were talking and laughing and splashing our feet in the water. One of us said a song lyric, and I started singing. And she started singing with me . . . and suddenly it was as if a little switch went off in her head. She stopped, looked around, and said, "People will hear us!"

That fear voice is the greatest hindrance to your creativity. What if I do or create something and someone thinks it's weird? What if they think it's bad? What if I feel stupid? What if this thing, this created thing that has come from my head and my brain and my heart, is rejected by everyone else? I see this fear rise up in accountants at times when we talk about a new kind of marketing effort. Posting more on social media. Writing blog posts. Sharing client testimonials. Recording video especially. It feels scary, like my friend's daughter glancing around to see who else might hear us singing. An element of this is based in professional care. You want to do good work, be the expert, and be seen for that. You want your prospective clients to be confident in you and your skills, not laughing at you or suspicious of you or doubting you.

You also know you are the expert in some areas. Your clients hire you for a reason. You know more about accounting and tax regulations (and often loans and grants and business recovery funding and payroll and other things) than they will ever know, and you're the one they come to. But the creative mindset, the creative project, goes deeper than facts or figures, and it touches the heart, the humanity. Sharing your creative ideas and efforts with the world means sharing a deeper part of you than you've been sharing before. And that can be scary.

It's also the very best thing you can do because people don't want "just an accountant" anymore. They can find one of those anywhere. They want the real you and your team. The ones they can have a coffee or a beer with, chat to about family life and hurts and pains and fears and losses and wins. The more you share of *that* you, the faster they will make the connection and decide you are the accountant for them.

The "what will people think" fear is almost always unfounded, but not because there won't be anyone who thinks it's weird. There probably will be a few of those. But the people who follow you, care about you, like what you like, value your opinion and expertise—those people will be open to whatever you want to share. Even if it's different or at first sort of strange. Because they like the real *you.* Sometimes, they're quicker to like the real you than you are.

And because you're not a celebrity and your posts and videos and social media haven't gone viral, no, the *entire world* is not looking at what you're sharing, saying horrible things, or turning you into a meme. After all, you're reading a book by someone whose first name has been turned into a meme and a joke. But I have a choice. I can let that bring me down, or I can let some people go ahead and use my name in vain while I pay more attention to what I have to say and get it out there. Those who know and like me and appreciate what I have to say love it no matter what my first name is. If you're worrying about the responses you're going to get, remember that the entire world isn't even aware of you. That can help you share whatever you want to share and be a tiny bit more creative. The people who like you already will like it. The people who don't will ignore it.

Many years ago, I was interviewed for an article on an accounting site. When the article came out, one of my comments was taken out of context. The resulting statement was quite a drastic one related to marketing. It wasn't accurate, but it also tapped into many accountants' fears about bad marketing, and I got a lot of very cruel comments on the post. Some of them were quite personal, taking digs at me and my experience and employment history, and almost all of them were completely dismissive of me knowing anything at all. It was the first time I'd had that happen, and for a few minutes, I was really crushed. I felt really stupid. I felt embarrassed that "all these people" thought I was a fraud. After I sorted through my embarrassment, I started to think. First, the statement wasn't even something I *had* said. So people weren't responding to something I actually believed or thought. And secondly, the kind of people who would say those kinds of things are not the kind of people I'd ever want to work with. I told the team about it, and one of them said, "Hey, you've arrived now! You've got haters!"

We laughed about that, and I realised he was quite right. You don't really get haters when you're not known, when you don't say anything dramatic, when you're not creative. And if you ever get to the point where there are some, by then, you have a big enough following of people who think so well of you that you will be defended and supported by your fans. And you genuinely won't care.

I still pay very close attention to what I say about creativity, about marketing, about accountants, and to accountants. As far as it depends on me, I want to live at peace and have a level of respect allocated to me. But I also want to share myself. I remember taking a visit to the Harry Potter studios in London, sharing some of that on Instagram, and having a moment like my twelve-year-old friend on the beach: *What if they think it's silly and childlike? What if they refuse to work with me or PF because of it?* Fortunately, I remembered the same counsel I give to our accountants when they're worrying about what others will think. I tell them, "Those who mind don't matter, and those who matter don't mind."

Actually, the opposite of my fears happens: My clients and team regularly send me links to Harry Potter memorabilia and crafts to make and locations to visit. They'll send pictures of their child's Harry Potter cake or a video of them reading from one of the books or curled up watching one of the films.

They'll try a sketch themselves because I'm always sharing sketches. They'll do something fun, something creative, something childlike. And they know I'll appreciate it because of what I've shared with them: myself.

What creative thing would you do or share if you weren't worried about what people would think?

Creativity involves emotions and feelings

When you're considering a new marketing approach, your questions reflect your wondering about how to prevent failure. What works? What doesn't? How much time do you and your team need to put in? When can you expect results? Those are good questions to ask, and any of us would ask the same of anyone in a professional service we were less familiar with.

Once you've started your marketing efforts, you start asking questions about your clients' experience, not just your own. How do my clients and prospects feel? What emotions are they experiencing when they review our marketing materials or our website? What are they worried about? What feelings are stirred up by my company's name or our colours?

Creativity has a lot to do with feelings, emotion, and experimentation. So does marketing. We try things to see if they work, not because we are guaranteed they will work. What seems to work for one accountant may completely fail for another. So stretching yourself in creative ways may feel uncomfortable. The good news is it's also strengthened by the use of systems and habits, which you are much more comfortable with. Let's talk about the systems you have and the ones you'll build which will bring out your natural creativity.

SECTION FOUR:

Getting started: finding your rhythm

4 GETTING STARTED: FINDING YOUR RHYTHM

BUILD CREATIVITY INTO YOUR WORK AND LIFE

You have an innate creativity. And at the same time, you have a resistance to it which is both built in and learned over time. Given that, leaning into your creativity means building small habits. Because creativity doesn't live to get results (remember Austin Kleon's story about his child drawing and then leaving those drawings behind to go do something else), it can be hard to understand the impact of building creative habits. But remember our definition of creativity includes problem-solving and curiosity. Building creativity may simply include noticing the problems you are solving in the day-to-day and being a little more curious about how you're doing that.

Jason Staats is someone many accountants point to as a shining example of a creative person. He tells me he "started very humbly"—the first step was wanting to learn more about email marketing. He had a little newsletter in 2019 that showed off new kinds of tech every week, and one week, he recorded a three-minute demo video to explain this tech. He reports the video was really bad . . . but he discovered that more people clicked on the video than anything else. He paid attention to that and started recording more video. During Covid, it was all hands on deck, figuring out how to get as much information out as possible using a one-to-many approach, and video became something of necessity. But ultimately his progress with video simply reflected a lot of work and many iterations. Jason says:

> In my opinion, creativity is work. When people point their finger and say, "Look at that person, look how creative they are," it's a way of putting people on a pedestal to make creativity feel unattainable or to be okay with not being like them. We label them unicorns, or creatives, and use that label to make the thing feel out of reach. Whereas the reality is, people in so-called "creative" domains are people who work hard and do that stuff a lot, and it's not sexy behind the scenes. A writer pumps out unbelievable words a day—but they did hundreds of those, which got them to the draft you think is so impressive. Like most things, creativity is about repetitions and doing it more than anyone else might think was reasonable.

Although you might consider certain types of work as falling into either a "creative" bucket or a "not creative" bucket, as an accountant, you do wildly creative things other people don't understand. It's simply that your subject matter is very technical. Perhaps you know tax law and also enjoy recording short videos while you're walking your dog, like Craig from Alchemy. Or you've spent time wiring up different apps to work together for the Managed Service Provider (MSP) market, like Paul from Red Earth CPA. This might not be framed as something people typically say is creative, but you're applying this kind of format to that technical thing people need to know about, and that's creativity.

"The reality is, there's a degree of things which do come naturally to folks, but especially once you get past a certain age, the continuous work you do will far surpass any sort of natural ability," says Jason. "That natural ability gets you so far, and then the question is, what are your systems?"

Let's look at the importance of building those systems, which I love to think about as rhythms.

The importance of building rhythm

Habits, or systems, help us achieve what we really want in life. In his book *Atomic Habits,* James Clear says he realised results weren't driven only by the goals he was setting; they were connected to the systems he followed. Those habits, those processes he followed day after day until he got to the result he was seeking for.

> *We think we need to change our results, but the results are not the problem. What we really need to change are the systems that cause those results.*
>
> —*James Clear,* Atomic Habits

You have options of how you might begin building a rhythm of creativity into your life. You could do something small every day, like setting a goal of writing two hundred words or even twenty words of a social media post. The habit itself is small, and you might expect small results. But this stage isn't about being obsessed with getting results; it's about sticking with the pattern, the rhythm. Part of creativity means you might not even know what your goal is yet, whether it's writing a book or publishing consistent blog posts on your website. It's okay to start a rhythm first and let the goal reveal itself. It's equally okay to set the goal first and choose a rhythm to help achieve that goal.

Part of creativity means you might not even know what your goal is yet.

The rhythm doesn't have to be daily, although those are the most powerful habits to build. You could connect your new habit to one you are already doing, one you do without even thinking about it. Every day you make coffee, check your emails, or take your children to school. Connecting your new creative habit to an existing one gives it a greater likelihood of success because you're always going to do that thing you *have* to do. You check emails so you get the information the client sent or the applications for the role you're hiring for. All of us have a time, a place, a way of checking these every day. For some, it's first thing in the morning. Or the moment we sit down at our desk. Or only at certain times of the day, so you can focus on getting work done. If your new habit is reading a chapter of a creative book, you could begin by reading that chapter before you open your emails. It will take a while to reset because the email habit is so automatic. You may have a few days or even a few weeks of opening emails, remembering the new habit, shutting down the emails, opening the book, and reading a chapter. That's okay. Building rhythms of creativity includes having patience and kindness towards yourself. This is new, this is different, and this may be uncomfortable. Most new habits are. For a while. Until they simply become your new way of doing things.

Creativity Exercise

Pick a habit you keep trying but failing to implement in your life. Look around at existing habits you are being consistent with. How can you attach this new habit to a tried and true one?

You can also choose to involve your team. Having accountability and community will give your new habits a greater chance of success. What could the whole team begin to do that would stir up creativity for the whole firm? You could choose a book and read it together with a defined deadline. I mentioned earlier that we often would read a book as a team in advance of a team retreat. I'd make sure we would have time to choose a book, share it with the team, give them time to buy it or download it, begin reading it consistently, and finish a week or so before the retreat began. When the deadline for having the book read was shared, everyone could easily calculate how many pages or chapters they needed to read per day, week, or month. We'd talk about progress in Slack, and the closer we got to the deadline, the clearer the habits became. One person needed to read a page a day to finish on time. Someone else needed to read a chapter a day. You could follow a similar process with recording videos or making lists of questions your clients ask or sharing favourite quotes from books and podcasts. It can be the simplest habit of all, but when you're all doing it together, someone is bound to remember on the day you forget and vice versa.

You can also make it a challenge. Doing a 100-day challenge is a great way to establish a new habit: Do the thing every day for one hundred days in a row. You could use this to write a certain number of words, record a video, or post on a social media platform. You could even connect a certain number of puzzle pieces in a puzzle you have sitting out on a table. If you find one hundred days is too much to start with, do a thirty-day challenge or even an eight-day challenge! The point is to set yourself a challenge which will push you a little and bring a sense of achievement. It's challenging (hence the name!) but not impossible.

When I decided to begin the 100-day video challenge for the third time (I'll share more about that later), Paul Redmond, an accountant in Ireland, saw my post and decided to join me. "At first I thought I did it simply because it was a challenge," he said. "But ultimately it was because I saw you were doing it, and I respect your opinion and approach. Video requires vulnerability, and that was a part of the challenge for me. But if someone I respect is showing up in that way, it feels safe for me to do it too." When I spoke with Paul about it, he told me about some of his other routines—one he set up in the mornings, and ten months on, he hadn't missed a single one. He also explained about a 100-hour challenge he intended to do next so he could become an expert in a specific area of tax. Completing a challenge is one of the simplest ways to settle into a rhythm.

With any habit you set, follow the Four Laws of Behaviour Change shared by James Clear in *Atomic Habits*:

1. Make it obvious
2. Make it easy
3. Make it attractive
4. Make it satisfying

When you do this, your habit will last, and your chances of reaching your goals will increase, not because you set a goal but because you built a rhythm which contributes daily and consistently to that goal. You might even find you enjoy the habit itself more than the resulting achievement. After all, once we achieve one goal, our mind is already leaping ahead to the next goal!

Small ways to build your creativity

Now that you've considered your rhythms, it's time to choose something to build your creativity on a consistent basis. Choose one of the areas in the list below or another one not listed. Choose something which can fit into your existing habits or which you've been meaning to do for some time and keep avoiding because it's more comfortable to do what you've always done (like checking your phone or replying to emails). We all know the results we get when we do what we've always done!

Writing: Choose an achievable (and slightly challenging) number of words per day to write. If you are not in the habit of writing at all, I'd suggest starting with two hundred. When I'm deep into writing for my next book, my daily word count is one thousand. At those times, I tend to write more on holidays and weekends, so it averages out on the busy days. I learned that was a good challenge number for me because it was hard enough to push me but not so hard that I gave up.

Videos: Record a certain length of video every day. This could be as little as ten seconds or as long as a few minutes. Using a social media platform like Instagram or TikTok can help simply for the practical exercise of tracking the length—the system will help you set the maximum of sixty or ninety seconds and will stop you when you've reached it. Even if you don't publish the video every day, getting into the habit of recording it and saving it as a draft will help for those days when you're not feeling very "creative."

Sketches: Whether you feel like you're artistic or not, a small sketch every day is a great way to stir up creativity. There are so many ways to approach it. You could choose a theme—

like animals, or trees, or names. You could niche down very specifically: one particular kind of animal or flower. One of my favourite ways to practise a sketch is to search on Google for the item I'm wanting to sketch using the word "icon" or "sketch" after it, depending on what level of detail I want. When you search for "shark icon," you'll get a very simplistic rendering of a shark which is simpler to copy. If you search "shark sketch," you'll get more detail. And if you search "illustration of a shark" or "painting of a shark," you'll get more detail still. Use pen and paper or your tablet and draw out the lines for whatever it is you're sketching that day. You could even set a timer and spend a maximum of five minutes on it. You might find you're extending the timer to finish your sketch! One of the things I enjoy about sketching is the way my mind is free to wander while I'm working on this one task. This also happens when I'm working on a puzzle or walking outside.

Walking: A short walk outside is one of the single best ways to let your mind float free if you approach it in the right way. You're not going to stir up creativity if you're making phone calls while you're walking or if someone else joins you and you're talking about life and work and family and whatever else comes to mind. Those are good things to do, but if you're walking to stir up creativity, it works best when you're on your own, there's no music or podcast or noise in your ears, and you're in a place of nature, like somewhere with woods or trees or water. I realise not all of you live in a place or have a life where that's easy to do. Maybe you have to drive to get to a place of nature. Maybe you don't have a car. Maybe you've got an illness or a health issue which prevents you from walking, right now or at all. The point is to get fresh air, get headspace, and do something which allows many thoughts and ideas to wander through your mind, ideally while your feet are wandering too. I am grateful to have woods and walking paths a few minutes from my front door, but I have those because every time I moved, I chose to buy my house in a place where walking paths were readily available. I've learned over the years when I'm grumpy or tired or feeling a distinct lack of creativity, even a fifteen-minute walk can clear the cobwebs and bring up ideas. I usually walk without music or any other noise, but I always carry my phone because that's when the ideas come. I'll think of a new product or service. A new section for the book I'm writing. An idea to discuss with one of the team. An idea for a story. If I haven't been in the habit of walking, it takes a while for this to happen. I'm merely focused on putting one foot in front of the other. But when I do it regularly, my feet can focus on the walking part, and my mind can do whatever it likes. Some days I come in from a walk with no notes, no new ideas, nothing ground-breaking. That's okay. Creative rhythms aren't about instant results.

Reading: Choosing a book and reading about a different aspect of creativity is a great way to stir that up. Here's a list of some of my favourites:

- *Steal Like an Artist: 10 Things Nobody Told You About Being Creative* by Austin Kleon
- *Show Your Work: 10 Ways to Share Your Creativity and Get Discovered* by Austin Kleon
- *Keep Going: 10 Ways to Stay Creative in Good Times and Bad* by Austin Kleon
- *Art & Fear: Observations on the Perils (and Rewards) of Artmaking* by David Bayles and Ted Orland
- *Atomic Habits: An Easy & Proven Way to Build Good Habits & Break Bad Ones* by James Clear
- *Creativity, Inc.: Overcoming the Unseen Forces That Stand in the Way of True Inspiration* by Ed Catmull
- *No Rules Rules: Netflix and the Culture of Reinvention* by Erin Meyer and Reed Hastings
- *The War of Art* by Steven Pressfield

- *Ego is the Enemy* by Ryan Holiday

These fall into the obvious category of creativity—the topics directly relate to the way we understand creativity. But you can also read books which look at things differently, something like *I Thought It Was Just Me (But It Wasn't): Telling the Truth about Perfectionism, Inadequacy, and Power* by Brené Brown, which talks about how perfectionism and inadequacy eat away at you and destroy your creativity with shame and judgement. Even a fictional story, if you usually read nonfiction, can stir up the tired recesses of your creative mind. (And the reverse is also true!)

Podcasts: Many of you regularly listen to business podcasts. Choose a podcast which is different from the kind you usually listen to or includes some aspect of creativity. Most of the authors listed above have their own podcast, and if they don't, it's almost a guarantee they'll have been a guest on someone else's podcast. One of my favourites is *The Futur Podcast* by Chris Do. Chris is an award-winning designer and CEO who founded online education platform The Futur, whose mission is to teach one billion people how to make a living doing what they love. His podcast explores how design, marketing, and business connect and overlap, and every episode gives me a new way of thinking about brand, that project I've been working on for ages, my writing, or something else. Another favourite is *The Tim Ferriss Show*, in which the host interviews people who are the best at something. It could be puzzles, weightlifting, recording music, acting, or sports coaching, but whatever it is, they've become the best at it, and he talks with them about their journey and what they've learned along the way. The episode with the puzzle expert was one of my favourites because I didn't even know being a puzzle expert was a thing. Now I think, *Well, of course it is*, because anything can be something you become the best at. But it gave me so many new insights into an area of expertise and creativity I'd never considered before. And I've gotten into the habit of having a puzzle on the table more often than not since then!

You could choose to do something different every day—that's creative too—but beware of the danger of not having a rhythm or habit for it. If your rhythm is to spend the first thirty minutes of every day in a creative exercise, you'll need a list of potential exercises to choose from or you're guaranteed to find yourself one morning thinking, *I have no idea where to start*, skipping the exercise entirely, doing the same the next morning . . . and you're right back to where you were.

Creativity requires structure: Rest requires work

You may still be thinking of creativity as something wild and untamed, like a small child flinging paint about with paintbrushes or with their hands. Or the wild-eyed and wild-haired writer frantically bashing away on an old battered typewriter in the back room of a (probably haunted) mansion. (With great quantities of whisky and cigarettes, of course.) There is an unplanned element to creativity which is fun and new and childlike. There is also a structure required to get to the best creative ideas.

One of the books our team read together was the previously mentioned book *Creativity, Inc.* by Ed Catmull, co-founder of Pixar. Something they instituted at Pixar is something they call Notes Day, which is like a big brainstorm, collaboration, ideas, thoughts, plans, actions day. It's a day to make the business better and to really listen to what the team have to share. As I was finishing the book in advance of a three-day team retreat, I read about Notes Day and realised the incredible amount of effort they put into preparing for this *one* day. Granted, they had over a thousand people at

Pixar, and, at the time, we had eleven people at PF, but still . . . it was Monday afternoon, and I was finishing the second half of a book I'd been telling the team to be sure to read for months.

I hadn't written the team retreat agenda. I hadn't given assignments or sent a prep video to the team yet. We all had a general sense of how it would run, but I hadn't lived up to my responsibility as a leader to prepare the crap out of this retreat so we were all excited and motivated and prepared and knew the boundaries and would get the most from it. The Pixar team prepared for months. Message boards, small groups, conversations, planning, assigning leaders, gathering input, documenting, listening. For *one day*. One really structured, organised, planned day to draw out creative ideas. And I started to see that in order to be creative, you need to structure things.

Rest is also an important part of retreats and of creativity itself. Every time I or the team plan to be away from client work for a retreat, we realise resting is *hard*. Choosing to take a break from our normal client work and have one-to-one conversations, think creatively, play, chat, brainstorm, get fresh air, think, read—well, none of that comes easy. It can be hard to be motivated or positive about taking time away because of how much work there is to do. It's tempting to use spare time on retreat days to finish client work and tell ourselves that's more restful in the end because then those projects would be off the very full list. And *then* we can rest. Although we know resting is good and helps us be more creative, it feels backwards to have to *work* at it. Surely resting just happens when you take some time off? We were tempted to redefine rest because of the work that never ends.

Whether you retreat on your own or with clients or with your team, it's an opportunity to remember that the work will never end, that choosing rest feels scary and hard, and we need it more than we know. Our clients will be okay (better, even) because we took the opportunity for a break to provide us creativity and rest.

Rest doesn't mean doing nothing. It doesn't mean sleeping and watching Netflix and sitting around. That's needed at times, but that's not rest. It's relaxation or recovery or entertainment. You're not thinking about anything (or you're letting something else fill your head so you don't have to think about something specific). Rest is a refreshment, a healer, a new perspective. And it requires preparation. Being clear about what rest includes and doesn't include. Choosing restful activities, like fresh-air breaks without phones or noise. Buying colouring books, painting materials, nice coffee, a journal, a nice set of pens. Brewing tea or making a really high-quality pot of coffee. Rearranging an area of your home or space to focus on resting.

Be aware that rest will bring out hard things. When you start resting, you're allowing yourself to think. To process. To consider. To wonder. To ask questions. To be challenged. You're not avoiding that thought or idea or concern; it's front and centre now (even if you didn't realise it had been pushed to the back), and your mind is clear enough to begin to consider it. That takes work too. The mental work of recognising these things will swirl to the top, and you're going to sit with them—not push them off by doing busy work like client emails and project management and the rush of daily life.

The outcome of creative time and resting time is new ideas. Changed plans. New perspectives. Redetermination.

To stir up creativity, you'll need to plan and create structure. And it takes work. But once you've done that, it becomes a place where the real good flows from. The outcome of creative time and resting time is new ideas. Changed plans. New perspectives. Redetermination. Over time, it also brings joy, refreshment, a lifting of the spirits, and a clear mind . . . all of which circle back to new creative ideas. And the cycle continues!

Creativity Exercise

Think about the last holiday you took where you felt truly rested. Make a list of three things you did while you were rested. How might you do one of these in a small way during one of the working days this week?

Moving from "hard work + yes" to "creativity + rest"

In the early days when you're getting started with a new business, you work hard and say yes to just about everything. Every enquiry, every client. Every invite to "pick your brain" or meet up for coffee and every request for a meeting. To be fair, in the early days, you say yes because there are things you haven't figured out yet. You don't have a specific, identified ideal client. You haven't carefully crafted a brand, including your style and tone of voice and imagery and message. Your services change with every request from a client. This works for a time, until you reach another level.

As time moves on, you adjust both your levels of hard work and how often you're saying yes. Instead of simply working hard at everything, you balance your creativity (the ability to see opportunity) with risk (the willingness to go for it). Instead of saying yes to almost everything, you begin to work on saying no to almost everything.

Most of us have done that. In my early days running PF, I said yes to any accountant who wanted to work with us with no qualifiers and no restrictions. I said yes to hiring outsourcers and freelancers, and later I said yes to hiring team members. I said yes to webinars and speaking engagements and events. I'd even say yes to speaking engagements which weren't for accountants or were on topics I was still figuring out. I remember spending a solid two to three days on preparation and travel and delivery of a talk at an event for people in the IT industry, and I wasn't even paid for it. (In shocking news, we got zero new business from that.)

I don't regret my yeses at that time because each yes taught me something. I learned about the kinds of accountants we were best placed to serve and those we weren't. I began to identify our company values and apply those to clients and team members. I learned about profitability when it comes to clients and services and team members. I learned which events and engagements were profitable and valuable for the business and for me and which ones were exhausting and didn't deliver much. I learned the toll taken on me by travel, events, and speaking. And I began to move slowly to a place of creativity and rest, of saying no to more things.

It's a process to make this shift, and it needs to be centred around what works for *you*. I practise "No-meetings Mondays," and have done this for years. It means saying no to any meeting, event, get-together, or deadline on a Monday. I know others who do this on a Friday or even two or three days a week. After all, the week will fill up with meetings if you allow it, seven days a week—eight, if it were possible. Beginning to say no is an opportunity to open up space for creativity.

Otherwise, it's just work, and work is endless.

I remember one of the toughest times in my business when

we'd had six team members leave in the space of six months, and I needed to pick up the slack with our monthly client meetings (which I didn't usually take). Some days, I had seven or eight Zoom meetings a day, plus all the other things I needed to get done. I seriously paused and thought, *What if I start taking meetings on Monday for a little while?* Whilst that was very tempting, I realised it wasn't the answer because eventually my Mondays would fill up just like the other days, and then I'd ask, "What about Sundays?" and before I knew it, I'd collapse. Work will always expand to fill your days, so it's your responsibility to block out the space you need—for rest, for creative headspace, for creativity to flourish. At the time of writing this paragraph, we're still in a very full time for my agency, but I'm sitting quietly in my yellow chair enjoying writing (with a nice cup of tea, or is it whisky?) because I stick to my "No-meetings Mondays".

You can still enjoy the fun, entrepreneurial aspect of risk; as your business grows and as you mature as a business owner, you learn your own strategies for mitigating that risk, as well as what an acceptable level of risk looks like to you. When you're considering a new idea and want to double-check the risk, a simple exercise is to consider the impact on your business in the primary categories of clients, team, finance, and operations. For each of these four areas, ask what the absolute best thing is that could come out of this new idea you're considering saying yes to. Then ask what the absolute worst thing could be. Say, for example, you're considering sending all your senior account managers to a week-long boot camp to train them in delivering advisory services. In terms of clients, the best-case scenario involves most of your clients signing up for more advisory services at a higher value. The worst case might involve no clients signing up for it. Or with the team, the best case might be a great deal of enthusiasm leading to increased productivity and efficiency, improving your profits. The worst case might be that a team member leaves because it's not the work they want to do. Reviewing the best and worst gives you a sense of risk and reward and helps you identify where to focus your creative energy.

As you practise your rhythms of creativity and choose rest to balance it out, you also need company along the way. Creativity needs space and quiet, and it also needs energy and ideas. You need the support of others as you build your patterns of creativity.

SECTION FIVE:

Getting help

5 GETTING HELP

CREATIVITY ISN'T (ONLY) A SOLO EXERCISE

Sometimes when I explain to a newfound friend that I'm an introvert, I get a look of surprise. This usually happens after we've had several hours of deep conversation or uproarious laughter and banter or after I've given a presentation on stage or regaled a group with stories. Explaining that my default preference is sitting quietly with a book or going on a long hike into the hills without meeting a single person all day is met with some incredulity. But the energy required for the deep or intense connections is fuelled by the times of quiet and headspace.

Creativity, too, has a strange dichotomy; it needs its own space, and it also needs company to thrive. As you're practising and honing your creative skills, you need a creative community to help keep those skills alive. We tend to emulate the people we spend the most time with. If everyone around you goes for a walk or a run or to the gym every day, it's far more likely you will too. If your family loves to play games or do puzzles, chances are they will be brought out at some point during any family get-together, and each of you will get better at them over time. The more you surround yourself with people who are stretching themselves creatively, the more likely you are to apply this to your business and life with increasing regularity.

Community helps in four different areas: consistency, contrast, collaboration, and coaching. We'll look at each of these areas in turn and then consider a few ways you can build this creative community for yourself.

Consistency in the same direction will bring your creative ideas to life. Keeping going is what gets you to that beautiful results stage you want. Consistency is also one of the hardest things to do on your own. Building a new habit is hard enough. Keeping that habit alive and going even on your hardest or most intense days is much harder. Having a community of people who are also striving (and struggling) means you don't feel so alone, and you're less likely to skip the consistency of your creative habit or work if you're around people who are also continuing to press on.

Contrast allows for a different perspective on the creative work you're doing. When you are around others who are building their own creative tools, systems, or teams, it opens up a window to what you're working on too. This isn't about playing the comparison game; the difference between comparison and contrast is in your perspective. Comparison means you're looking at their work and looking at yours and coming to the conclusion that theirs is better. Contrast means you're looking at their work and seeing your own in a different way. When I've watched a film or read a book I appreciate, I try not to say, "That was good!" Referring to a creative work as "good" or "bad" moves it out of a creative environment and into a decisive one. And a decisive environment has no room for questions, doubts, curiosity, or perspective. Maybe I did like this particular painting, but equally, someone else didn't like it.

Instead, I say what I appreciated about it or what it brought up for me.

I remember visiting the Scottish National Gallery and coming across a painting called *The Skating Minister* by Henry Raeburn. It depicts a man in minister's garb—black clothing and a black hat and a little white collar—skating, arms folded, on a frozen loch. I remember standing in front of that painting for some time because it stirred up quite a lot for me. I was struck by the dichotomy of something as joyful and freeing and open as ice skating contrasted with the restrictive, dark, even foreboding attitude of the minister himself. His arms are folded, his face is serious, but his legs are moving in an almost graceful way. It feels like at any moment he will either release his arms and move freely and joyfully or stop skating and stand there, cold and shivering and miserable on the ice. The contrast makes it fascinating. You wonder what's going on there, and you don't have the whole story, so you contribute some of your own story as you experience it.

I'm not a painter myself, but I enjoy doing sketches and drawings. If I were to compare my work to that of Raeburn (no relation that I know of!), I could feel my work was lacking. Childlike. I use bright, thick lines to give an impression of something; he uses detail and can draw people's faces. He is a master and I am . . . not. But the point isn't to compare my work with Raeburn's; it's to appreciate the contrast and learn something or experience something. When you compare your creativity or the work you're engaged in with another business owner or accountant, the point is not to figure out whose is "better." It's to experience the contrast and see what it brings up for what you're working on. Looking at someone else's work can be helpful. Looking at it to compare yourself or your work in a negative way isn't as helpful.

Cheryl Sharp, an accountant near London, used to play the comparison game in many areas of marketing but especially with video. She'd find herself looking at others' Instagram reels, thinking, *Oh, they're so good,* and she'd end up recording nothing. "If I delve deeper, it wasn't about the reel itself," she said. "It was the fact that they were doing it, and I wasn't. Here was yet another thing I wasn't doing, something to add to my already overwhelmed plate." It was a mindset thing. "When I'm in a 'down' mindset, everything is a comparison. *That person is doing better than me. I couldn't record a reel like that. There's no point in trying.* But when I'm in a positive space, I see things more as inspiration." And the number one thing that moved her out of the comparison space was asking for help from her team. "Seeing the team do their own videos gave me confidence to do mine," she said. "Instead of trying to mentally prepare for all the moving parts—ideas, recording, editing, publishing—I got a list of videos I could record and just did that part. Then I got help with the rest."

Collaboration brings community into your creative work. The ideas and feedback of others are brought in so the entire burden of creating the new thing doesn't weigh entirely on your shoulders. Some of the ways collaboration can show up include idea generation, review and feedback, and sharing your work.

At the idea generation stage, you're connecting with others because you feel a bit stuck. Or you want to make sure you're considering every angle. Our marketing director at PF does this when she's planning one of our events. She's got a theme and a rough idea for the day, but she wants suggestions different from her own. So she has a quick chat with me or one of the team, and within a few minutes, she's either stretched the original ideas she had, or we've come up with new ones she hadn't thought of before. Idea generation can be as simple as messaging someone to say, "I was thinking about how I might launch this new service—got any ideas?" Or it can be as intense as blocking out a full day or even weekend with several others to dig into your launch, consider how it might work, and decide whether it's worth pursuing.

Review and feedback mean you have a solid draft or something nearly ready to share, and you want new eyes on it, usually to see what you're missing (or could be missing). This could be a detailed review, such as spotting spelling mistakes or noticing that an aspect of the design is tilted when it needs to be straight. It could also be a conceptual review, such as sharing whether this thought leadership article makes sense and will be appealing to the audience it's meant to reach. When asking for feedback, be specific about what you want, and ask people you trust for their expertise and judgement in the area you need. If you share a link to an article you've written and ask for feedback, most people will tell you, "It's great!" You'll feel good about yourself, and they'll feel like they've helped you, but really you haven't gotten any feedback at all. It's similar to that concept of saying a book is good or you liked a painting at a museum. You haven't given them anything besides a vague sense of pleasure in something, and this sense may colour their view of it or prevent them seeing it with their own unique perspective. Ask for what you want. Let's say you've written an article for the owners of tech start-ups. The very best kind of feedback is going to come from someone who owns a tech start-up or at the very least knows people in that category and knows what they want or wonder or need. Share the link with them and ask specific questions, such as "Is there anything in here you didn't know already?" or "What points do you relate to, if any?" Asking "what"-based questions help them give a specific answer.

It's okay for your creative work not to land with the whole world. The important thing is for it to land well with the world you are trying to reach.

Sharing your work with your creative community allows you to do a test run before you publish or post this creative thing you've been working on. We have a Marketing Lab community, a place for accountants we're working with who chat to us and each other. In Lab, people share something they're working on—an article draft, a video script or a first effort at a video, or a sketch they've made of a particular process within their business. They explain what they've created and why and who it's for and get input from others who are creating similar things in their own businesses. One accountant may show a sketch of their onboarding process, and another accountant who already has their process documented might reply with a link to their website page or onboarding guide or designed image showing the path. At this stage, you're opening yourself up for idea generation, review, feedback, and opinions all at once, but you're doing it in a small way before you release it to the rest of the world. And don't panic about letting "the whole world" see it; your world is going to be small at the start, so you'll get mostly positive responses from people who already know and trust you. Remember that once you get to the stage of having haters, you'll also have your fans. Your community, your people who want to be part of what you're creating. Not everything is for everyone, and not every person is for everyone. It's okay for your creative work not to land with the whole world. The important thing is for it to land well with the world you are trying to reach.

Creativity Exercise

Choose something you've been working on and have excitement about but haven't shown anyone yet. Share it with your mastermind, marketing community, or a group of like-minded business owners and ask for feedback. Don't feel obliged to implement all their suggestions, but look for patterns of something you might have missed seeing.

Coaching is the final element of your creative community. This may be one-to-one or group coaching, and it provides a different perspective to the things you've been getting from those who are like you. A coach, or a coaching group, is going to understand who you are and what you're trying to do; they're also going to care enough to push you beyond what feels comfortable. Everyone I know who has pushed themselves to something new (or different or scary) has eventually involved a coach to do it successfully. The person who has been running every day and wants to run an ultra or finish a 50K or a 100K race. The client who has been writing blogs for years and decides it's time to write a book. The team member who is seeking a promotion and needs to build their skills to reach it. The coach is someone who has been there, done that; they've run the 50K, they've published the book, they've been promoted themselves. They take their learnings, sometimes put them into a structured plan or methodology, and help you apply those to your particular situation.

Finding a coach can be a little like finding the right therapist. You may have to try working with several different people until you find the one who is the right fit for you. It's your decision, and this coach needs to fit with the right motivation style for you. Some people do best with the hard-line coaches, those who talk fast and take no shit and won't let you off with anything. This person might lean towards the drill sergeant attitude: "I don't want to hear 'no,' private! Get down and give me two hundred push-ups! Now!" Other people are more motivated by a gentler, more patient approach: someone who listens and asks questions and lets you get there in your own time. They might even leave it to you to build your own structure or habits rather than telling you which ones to use. It's okay to work with one person or company, decide on reflection they're not a fit for you, and then try another. If you do that, be sure to ask yourself what exactly wasn't a fit. A simple "Nah, I wasn't feeling it" could be correct, but why? Were they too pushy or not enough? Did they leave you to lead the conversation so much you felt like you were coaching yourself? Was the structure *too* structured? The more specific you are about what didn't work for you, the more information you have to find out what will work next time.

To build your creative community, you have a few choices. You can self-select your own group. Identify the people you most admire for their creative traits—problem-solvers, question askers, habit makers, community builders—and build an internal system of getting or staying in touch with these people on a consistent basis. This is the hardest way to build community because the full weight of the responsibility sits with you. If you're having a hard day (or week or month or season) or the busyness of life and work is overwhelming, connecting with other creative people may be the last thing you want to do in that moment. When I made the decision to finish the content for this book by setting and building the daily habit of writing a thousand words a day, I remember telling a fellow writer about it. "Wow . . . that's amazing!" she said. "First, well done, you. That's so dedicated and focused. And second . . . fuck you." I completely understand the feeling. When someone else is absolutely nailing something you're not really focused on right now, you are equally amazed and impressed, and you may also feel slightly annoyed. Why are they being so awesome and achieving so much? Why did you stay up watching yet another Netflix episode and have to drag yourself out of bed in the morning while this other person is up with the birds and off for a morning run? But that's the comparison game. Ideally, your community includes a mixture of people: those who are up and at 'em early doors and those who slept longer.

If you decide to self-select your creative community, you'll need to use your rhythms (or build a new rhythm) to make sure you stay connected with others who will spur you on, stir you up, remind you of what's important, and be there for you on a hard day.

Another option is to join an existing creative community. This may be the easiest and simplest choice for most of you, which is why so many of these exist. Find the group best suited for you personally and try not to overthink it. As with choosing a therapist or choosing a coach, you could spend months trying to find the perfect one, or you could find one who seems pretty good and give it a go. The worst that happens is you realise it's not a fit and move on. One of the easiest groups to find is the community which has built up around an author (or has been crafted by the author to bring these people together).

When James Ashford created the GoProposal app, one of the first things he did was to build a Facebook community for accountants and bookkeepers using the tool. In those early days, I was given access to that group, and I remember seeing endless conversations which were curious and open, reflecting James's positive approach. Everyone in it was an accountant, and they all had the same ability to understand each other's situations, ask for advice, and share victories together. After a time, the business was sold, and the group changed too, but in those early days, it provided the community accountants needed. The Agencynomics group was a community of agency owners with a subgroup specifically for female agency owners. I used the app to ask questions, answer questions, and see what other agency owners were discussing or dealing with. Every once in a while, I'd go down to London or travel to Edinburgh for an agency owners' lunch or dinner and spend time hearing ideas, sharing stories, making and receiving suggestions. Every time I would come back feeling like at least one thing I'd been blocked by was now opened up a little. Even if I didn't feel too inspired at a particular time, I had the opportunity to be the inspiration for someone else, and that in itself is motivating.

Pick an author or speaker you know and admire, and look for the community they've built. It might be an intentional one, like a group you join or even pay for, and it might be an organic one that has grown up naturally around them. Join it, and, most of all, make a conscious effort to be a part of it. Write an introductory message. Read others' messages and comment on them. Ask for help from those who are further on their journey than you are. Look for ways to be of help to those who are just getting started. To be part of the PF Community, go to wearepf.com/marketing-lab and sign up!

You can also feel the benefit of community by being surrounded with one, even if it's not something you're officially part of. Going to a coffee shop or a library or even a museum surrounds you with people who are being creative in some way, just like you are in that moment. When I want to make progress on one of my books, I often block out a day and go somewhere else besides my home office. Before I moved to the island which is now my home, I'd go to my local Starbucks and choose the comfiest seat with a view towards all the other people coming and going all day. On the Isle of Mull, I can still get a different perspective by driving to a café on a farm. There's a long winding table alongside a huge picture window, and I can look out to the fields and mountains while writing. I can order incredibly good coffee and cakes and soup for lunch, and either watch the people coming and going or disappear into my own little world. In the space of four or five hours, I can achieve more than I'd ever have done in my usual work environment. Taking ten minutes to research a few places available to you in your local area—or even selecting one which isn't local at all and making a real effort to get there—can help you be surrounded by others who are doing *something* creative; you might not even know what it is. You may not need to know. It's possible you'll get into conversation with someone and be inspired to new ways of living or working, and it's equally possible you'll speak to no one else but the barista and still come away inspired.

Sometimes the mere act of being open and curious will bring you a little slice of community when you least expect it. I was walking to the train station one morning, and an older gentleman was about to pass me on the left, so I glanced over and said good morning and commented on the beautiful day. He commented back, and we started chatting. Five minutes later, I find myself striding along with Jim, hearing some of his life story and the countries he loves and the photography degree he got in another time of his life. To this day, I'm still impressed by his story about how he took a month to create a photography project in Vietnam, only to discover his project didn't fit the qualifications required by his degree, so he packed up and drove the NC500 route in Scotland and redid the entire project on that road trip. Here was someone a good twenty years older than me, and not only was he walking faster than I was, he didn't allow failure to get him down. He got the project wrong, so he picked another and started again. And he didn't consider the long journey to Vietnam to be a waste; it was creative input, it was a different perspective, and it was a worthwhile exercise in and of itself.

Reading books and watching documentaries and observing others will stir you up creatively. Having a community of people who get how you feel and are able to help weigh in on the hard days will help keep you going. Creativity may be a solo exercise at times, but community makes sure you don't give up along the way. But even with all of this support, there are times where nothing seems to work.

Creativity may be a solo exercise at times, but community makes sure you don't give up along the way.

WHEN YOU'RE STUCK: MOVING THROUGH CREATIVE BLOCKS

Sometimes, no matter how determined or motivated you are or how many books you read on the topic or podcasts you listen to or rhythms you try to build, you just get . . . stuck.

Nothing is vibing. Your brain isn't braining, and the creativity isn't creating. When I set my goal of one thousand words a day to finish this book, I also set a "hard day" target, which was two hundred words. I recognised the reality of life and the reality of my life and my patterns. Remember my fellow writer who was both admiring me and annoyed by me and my daily word count? I told her, "Go ahead and be impressed now because I know myself. I know there is a day or a streak coming where I'm going to struggle and possibly even give up entirely." *That* is what I'm trying to build a habit against. I do great for a while, but to continue to the end is tough. When I was typing this chapter, I was on a sixteen-day streak. I hadn't hit the hard day yet. When I did the self-review of the whole book and worked on the edits for this chapter, I was in a tougher place and not keeping to my rhythms of writing or editing or even swimming regularly. I had to go back to the hard day target, sometimes for many days in a row. You never know when you might need it, but I've had enough knocks to my mental and creative health to know about the times of walking through creative sludge.

The first way to arm yourself against these times is to *recognise they exist.* This may seem obvious. I doubt anyone reading this is thinking, *Oh, I will never skip my creative rhythms, ever*. You're realistic enough about yourself and about how the rhythms of life go to know things go in waves and in seasons. Better yet, you're the best person in the world to recognise how they show up in your life specifically. Knowing life will happen and you'll be thrown off your rhythms is one thing; knowing how and when you get thrown off and what your patterns are for dealing with it is another.

My rhythm disruption happens when there's a personal struggle or a grief to go through. It could be something which simply happens to me, like when I fell whilst hiking and broke my ankle. It could be someone else's choices affecting me, like when we need to let a team member go. And it could be my own choices, like realising an organisation I was part of was toxic and unhealthy and I needed to leave. All of these and others have had an impact on my ability to stay focused or motivated.

I was about to say motivation isn't a magical thing we can summon to us whenever we want, but perhaps that's the point. Motivation is rather magical, and *because* of that, we aren't able to summon it whenever we want. One of my favourite parts in the first Harry Potter book is when Harry gets to Hogwarts and realises magic isn't a matter of waving a wand around and saying some words. There's work involved. He attends classes and learns history and is given spells, and he has to practise. Over and over. He has good days and a lot of really bad days. Motivation, like magic, has to be practised. And worked at. And it doesn't always come when called. You may need to put yourself in the right place or space for creativity to show up.

Creative headspace

Summoning creativity may not be a matter of magic or even sheer will, but it can come nearer and more frequently when the space is right. The concept of creative headspace includes the kind of room you need for your mind, your brain, your energy to do its best work. It includes rhythms and rest; it's both physical and mental.

Everyone's creative headspace will show up differently. One accountant told me, "Being quiet at home doesn't work for me. I'll get up, I'll put the washing out, I'll do little tasks. But if I'm in a noisy coffee shop, I'll put my earbuds in and suddenly I feel more inspired. The noisier, the more chaotic environment, the more focus. It's like I reverse the surroundings and fight to create some of my own quiet around it."

Another accountant, Randy, has a different kind of headspace entirely. "For me, it's hanging out with others—that's where I learn the most and get the most creative. In a loud place with others where we're talking and I'm learning from them—that's where I get my information and knowledge. I probably go to fifteen or twenty conferences a year, and I just love that space. I see how people approach things differently, and that's my fuel."

For me, depending on the kind of progress I need to make, it's either collaboration or quiet. Collaboration is for budding new ideas, wonderings, questions, and challenging everything. I get this collaboration through team or client retreats, events, conferences, workshops. Then when it's time to consider, to gather, that's when I need quiet, the deep level of quiet which goes down to my soul. It usually takes days, sometimes even a week to get to the deepest level of quiet, but I'll take smaller amounts whenever I can plan for them.

It may look like working from the same home I always work from, the same office room . . . but I'm sitting in the big yellow chair with a footstool, working on my laptop rather than at the main desk with the big monitor. Like Mr. Keating standing on his desk, I'm changing my perspective and looking at things a different way. I'll drive down the road to my favourite café, the one with the long winding tables and the big picture windows looking out to the mountains and the sea. Or when I'm traveling to a conference, I pick a co-working or remote working space and plan projects to work on from that different perspective.

Whether it's a café, a co-working space, a new city or simply a new chair, choosing your version of creative headspace opens your mind up. How you approach the hour or the day or whatever time frame you've set aside will again depend on what works best for you. One of the most productive days of creative headspace I had whilst working on this book was a blocked-out day surrounded by an extremely full calendar on either side. I had a few days with nine or ten meetings in a row (usually my absolute limit is six, and even five is pushing it). I had a board meeting coming up, which always meant more prep and more thinking time and more gathering of data and holding of pre-board-meet conversations. We had a team member visiting from the States and some team get-togethers, and everything was go. But amongst all this activity my one blocked-out day stood like a sentinel in my calendar. I protected it. I allowed a few meets, but they were by old-fashioned phone call instead of video call. I sat in my yellow chair with the laptop. I took breaks. I read portions of creative books. I thought. The accountants who had booked interviews were each a few hours apart, so I'd hold one interview and then have plenty of time to review the notes, gather my thoughts, and work on another one of these sections before the next interview. Sometimes I'd get distracted from working on the actual writing and typing and editing, but even then, it was a creative distraction. I'd record a video or clips for a reel we were creating. I took a walk in the woods, quietly, without AirPods or phone.

Creative headspace isn't only about having time and space to work on things you want to achieve; it's about getting to *who* you most want to be. At one of the client retreats I held, we each wrote down notes on who this person would look like. For me, it includes being rested and having freedom of time and the mental and emotional space to connect with others and see them become the best of who they can be. It includes abundance and the opportunity to be generous with my time and resources. That's what creative headspace delivers for me. And if it delivers a book or a video course or a new guide or a new service offering at times, so much the better.

Sometimes, no matter what you do, you're just not feeling it. You've taken the space, but your head feels blank. You rested, you ate well, you drank water, you changed locations, you tried to open yourself up creatively, but motivation isn't just elusive, it's invisible. When this happens, you may need to summon its lesser-known counterpart, which is manufactured motivation.

Summoning manufactured motivation

Manufacturing motivation involves recognising that motivation itself is not going to come when called. You're going to have to drag that shit out, possibly kicking and screaming at first, like a small child who refuses to go to bed. Remember my story about needing to record multiple videos when I wasn't in the mood? The vibes weren't vibing, and the videos weren't videoing, and *I did not want to do it.* And equally, I needed to. I had a deadline from our marketing team, and I had an example to set for the rest of our team, who were also recording their videos. I solved it by recording the video which needed the most energy, the most enthusiasm and positivity. It was a video for the team to announce we'd reached our revenue target for the year and they were all getting a bonus. Deep down, I was pleased about this and happy for the team. But if I had recorded the video then, it would have been the most boring and angry video ever, which would destroy the whole point. I knew the enthusiasm was there, somewhere. It was simply refusing to be summoned. I decided to help myself manufacture enthusiasm by playing music. I found songs about money that I played (loudly) as I planned out my video. And then . . . the magic arrived. I remembered that scene from the film *Love Actually* where the guy tells the girl he loves her by showing her a series of messages handwritten on paper signs that he flicks through while Christmas carols play in the background. So I looked for a doorbell sound and played that, then played the money song, and walked the team through the update on our revenue targets and their bonus through a series of messages written on paper signs. It was simple. Once I'd finished, it was actually fun. I'd enjoyed making it, I felt proud of it, and the team had a great time watching it and laughing and appreciating both it and the message about the bonus. Creativity had been there all along, but it took effort for it to come out. I had to manufacture the motivation at first.

Once I'd finished that video, it was much easier to do all the others. That's another thing about motivation—it may need to be nurtured at first, but once it comes, it flows faster and faster. It's like a river which has been dammed up for a while. At first, you pull out a little stick which has been blocking the flow. A trickle starts to come out, and you realise there's a larger stick, maybe even a big log, stuck in there. You reach in and pull that out, and before you know it, the whole barrier has broken apart, and the water is flowing now, bigger and faster, and before you fully realised it was possible, you have a waterfall of motivation and creativity.

I don't like the phrase "Fake it till you make it," because I don't like anything fake. I value honesty and integrity and reality. But the beauty of manufactured motivation is that the motivation itself and the creativity within you aren't fake at all. It may *feel* fake to play music and dance about a bit when you're feeling grumpy and annoyed, but the reality is something good is there, hidden or misunderstood or lost, and part of your creative job is to seek it and find it. Let the reality of your creative self come out.

Everyone will have different creative blocks. Yours will not be like mine. Some people go through times of personal grief or pain and find those are some of the most motivated times of their life. You need to know what your creative blocks are and identify them in the quiet times, the good times, the creative times. Once you've identified them, you can begin to build a plan for what your hard day looks like. And give yourself room for the hardest of times. There will be periods of your life which involve something so serious you simply need to survive. When I broke my ankle, it wasn't merely the broken ankle itself which was hard. I'd been hiking alone in a remote place on an island and had to bum-shuffle down a ravine for an hour and a half to get to a place where I could call for help. It was winter, and the sun was going down fast, and I was in danger of being very cold very fast. The local coast guard came with a helicopter and flew me to a hospital on the mainland. I needed to get myself out of the hospital and then to my home hundreds of miles away in the middle of the night. Once I got home, I was navigating things like stairs and toilets and the fact that I'd forgotten to put the sheets on my bed before I left on the trip.

Every little thing wasn't just hard; it felt impossible. For the next month, I was in survival mode. Getting up in the morning, going downstairs, and making coffee and breakfast took two hours every day. Making a cup of tea was a massive effort. The first time I took a shower by myself, I had to rest in bed for the remainder of the day. We all have had seasons in our life which require survival mode—a broken relationship, a divorce, a surgery, a family member in hospital. When those seasons come, it makes sense to chuck literally everything out the window and just make it through.

The good news is your creativity and your motivational energy haven't died. They've simply been set aside, and when you're ready, you can pick them up again. I moved from survival season to healing season back to motivated season eventually, and you will too. That's when you pick up your rhythms again or create new ones, and you see the barriers begin to break apart and the motivational waters start flowing again.

When they do start flowing again, everything seems to be working brilliantly, almost on its own. Like what Matthew McConaughey calls "green lights" in his book of the same name, it's as if you are driving and every light you come to is green. The way is opened before you, and it feels like the whole world is for you. Days when you're seeing results from your efforts, and everything feels worthwhile.

The challenge with the type of day you're having is that you never know what kind of day it is until it's over. When I look back, I see good days, slow days, hard days, big days, and victory days. *Good days* are when everything is working as you expect. You wake up on time, your coffee machine works, you follow your creative rhythms, you tick things off your to-do list. You might even have a small win or an achievement along the way, like reaching a partway target. On *slow days*, you're still progressing, but nothing feels exciting. Things are a little weary, and you're in turtle mode: slow, steady, careful, nothing wild. *Hard days* are tough. You've been up sick all night, or your kids have, and you're utterly exhausted. You've had bad news from a family member or friend, and it's on your mind, and everything is distracted. On hard days, you know it will pass, but you also recognise it's affecting you in a fairly significant way. *Big days* are the opposite of that. On big days you are sailing—everything is working, you're getting loads done, you're surpassing targets. And *victory days*, which are rarer, are when it all comes together into some kind of recognition. The big client signed the huge proposal. Your book was published, or your podcast launched. You hired your first team member. Your physio signed you off, and that part of the healing is done.

I remember my sister telling me about a day when her kids were young and they went to the local country fair. Rides, candy, sunshine, petting animals, playing games—they were living their best lives. Towards late afternoon, they got ice cream, and my niece was about to taste her ice cream cone when it slipped and fell and lay there melting on the ground at her feet. "This is the worst day *ever*!" she cried out . . . and my sister was trying not to laugh because it had been the best day ever, just with one spilled ice cream cone. But as an adult, when you come up against the thing that might tip you over the edge—your melted ice cream—you can know what to do with it. Some days you laugh at yourself and buy another. Other days, you leave it there and decide it's time to go home.

You don't necessarily need to wake up in the morning thinking, *Ah, today is a hard day* or *Today is a slow day*. I've had many days I genuinely felt were going to be slow, and I followed my rhythms and habits, and before I knew it, the day was moving into a good day or even a big day. The reality of big days is that often the things you've been working on slowly, day after day in turtle mode, can turn around at any moment and come through for you. Green lights all the way. But consider this: Are you calling it a hard day because you had one hard thing? Are you choosing for it to be a slow day when you could power through? Only you really know the answer to that.

On days when all the ideas are bubbling, make notes. Capture ideas, write down bullet points, sketch out diagrams, start a slide deck. Whatever way you can capture these good things, get them down, and save them for the slow and hard days. I use the notes app on my phone, categorised into different areas like the different books I'm writing or a guide I'm writing for our agency or notes on our sales process. Every time I have an idea or a thought or a few points I know I could expand on, I get those down—and I almost always have my phone with me so they're not lost. Often this happens when I'm out on my daily walk. When my feet are moving automatically along the path, my mind is free to let the thoughts and ideas stir and simmer. The very section of the book you're reading now about the kind of days you experience came from notes I made on a Sunday afternoon when out for my walk. On Monday morning, when creativity felt low and I didn't have much energy, I had the foundational elements, the bare bones, to begin with. You can still use the energy and motivation of a good day to write or create or publish, but be aware there are other kinds of days coming. It's like meal prepping when you know you have a lot on in the coming week. Chopping the carrots and onions and potatoes so you have them ready and can make a big batch of soup the moment you need to. Cooking your own chicken or vegetable stock and freezing it so it's ready to use in a variety of recipes. The small amount of prep one day means you're supported on another day. It's almost as if your former self is coming through for you in that moment: "Oh look, Former Me was ready for this! What a relief."

You might even decide that for you, there are only good days and victory days, and you allow yourself a hard day only a rare once in a while. I know people who approach life like that. I honour it and respect it. However you approach it, recognise that creativity doesn't flow endlessly like a stream. It comes and goes, turns on and off seemingly at a whim, and can be really hard to measure. Get to know your own kinds of days. You could even start tracking them alongside your creative rhythms to look for patterns. It's in looking back you gain an understanding of how you've been approaching things. And then you ask the question *How is that working for me?* Is there anything you need to change?

Changing things can feel a fairly simple, if not easy, task to approach. Changing yourself and your mindset, however, can be another challenge entirely. Like going to a therapist for the first time.

MARKETING THERAPY

"I'll do the math, but I'm not meeting with a fucking therapist."

This quote is from one of my favourite films of all time, *Good Will Hunting*. Here's a young, clever mathematical genius named Will who, up till now, has only stuck with what he knows. What he's easily good at. He's got hurts and pains and issues and distrust and fear, but in his mind, he doesn't need help with any of those. He has his friends, he knows what he enjoys, and if he needs to beat someone up who disrespected him in some way, so be it.

Until it lands him in court and potentially in jail. A maths professor sees his potential and offers to work with him but insists he needs to see a therapist as part of the deal. No way, says Will. With maths, he knows the answer instantly or very quickly. He knows how to get there. But the idea of meeting with a therapist hits a road block; he won't even consider it. It turns out this is because in therapy, he doesn't know the answers. When the therapist digs deep and asks questions he's never considered before, leading to uncomfortable truths . . . he backs away. He'll do the math, but he's not going to meet with a therapist.

If you've seen the film, you know he does eventually see the therapist. But it takes many different meetings and many different therapists (some of whom storm out in anger) before he meets with one who actually talks his language. Asks the right questions. Listens. Leaves space.

As an accountant, you may feel the same when it comes to marketing and to the creativity which sits at the heart of your identity. You're used to having all the answers or getting to them quickly. You're a numbers person, not a words person or a therapy person. You don't want to talk about it or dig into what's holding you back; you want to *get stuff done* and, most of all, get results. Like Will, you don't want to do anything which feels uncomfortable or confusing. You like having the answers. You'll do the marketing, but you're not really interested in digging into why this one worked and why that one didn't. You're not interested in marketing therapy. You just want someone else to make sure it gets done: "I'll do the marketing, but I'm not going to be a fucking creative."

"Just tell me what to do," you say. "If you say I need to write blogs, I'll write blogs! Okay! Record video? Ugh, I guess so . . . why do I have to do this? Just tell me the answer!" But marketing itself doesn't have the answers pat and ready. You do. They're in your head, in your past experiences, in your expectations and the very heart of who you are as a person and as a business owner.

You can't just "do the math" or do the technical actions. You have to dig deep. Only then will your marketing reflect who you truly are, and your prospects will see that truth and love it. Anything less than that confuses them and delays your results and wastes everyone's time.

So many accountants who have gone through the Foundational sessions we do with every client have said, "Those are really good. But hard. Like therapy!" When you're reviewing the clients you want to serve, your purpose and values, why you do what you do . . . it goes deep. To lean into the marketing therapy element, you need to dig deep. Digging deep means some or all of these things:

Being asked the hard questions. What's almost hilarious about this is that the hard questions end up being something like "How are you?" or "And how did that make you feel?" or "And is that working for you?" I say they're hard questions, but in reality, it's what the question brings up. It may be the fact you haven't really allowed yourself space to answer those questions before. You rush, you hurry, you answer emails, you get your daily work done. But sitting quietly in a room with no music and no podcasts and no bustling activity (either the family or the business), with all the space to consider whether this thing is actually working for you . . . that's what makes it hard.

One of the Foundational sessions we deliver with accountants covers their branding. The questions in this session vary depending on who we're working with and how much work they've done already on their audience, their values, their philosophy and mission. One session I had with two owners, Jon and Meghan, dug really deep into the values. They knew exactly who they were and who they wanted to work with but had never documented it in the way we were about to. Afterwards, Jon sent us a note to tell us how he felt about that session:

> Hey, just a quick note of thanks. I have never, in my entire career, had anyone ask the questions you've asked us over the

> past few sessions. Not only do I feel this tremendous sense of relief that someone gets what we do, but I also feel a sense of gratitude that you care enough to ask these questions to help us build what I know will be a brilliant new identity and presence. I can't thank you enough. I purposely left my day light today because of our meeting, but I'm also glad that I did. I can take some time and just sit with everything we discussed today. I had high hopes when we started this engagement; now I know those hopes have ground in which to plant roots and grow.

I was going to say find someone who can ask you the hard questions. But "find someone who" is one of my least favourite phrases ever. It can be really hard to "find someone who." It's the sort of thing people say when their partner has surprised them with a trip for a big birthday, and they say, "Find someone who takes you to Paris." Like, bully for you, but if I could do a quick search online and find someone who is exactly the partner or therapist or team member or client I need, I would. Part of the hard work is finding someone, which means you're going to need to try a variety of people and companies. If you resonate with the principles in this book (and my first book too), you can go through the Foundations sessions with me or one of the strategists on my team. And if you're not ready for that, you can start small by booking a few marketing therapy sessions with me. I'll ask the hard questions and give you space to consider them. And if those aren't what you need, that's absolutely okay. Keep searching. I'll even help you look.

Letting it simmer. When there are deep questions to consider, you're not going to know the answer straight away. Maybe even at all. It could be there's no right or wrong answer; there's just something else for you to try or consider. Whatever the question is—whether it's about the kind of audience you serve or the messaging on your website or why you're running this business at all—take time to consider your thoughts about it. My family makes a hot apple cider at Christmas time which is at its best when it's been in a slow cooker all day long. We put in apple juice, an orange stuck with cloves, some mulled wine spices, a cinnamon stick, and a handful of sweets called Red Hots. They're hard cinnamon sweets that dissolve over time. A long time. Because we're all together for a few days or even a week, we make this hot cider on day one and leave it in the slow cooker and keep it going, topping it up with more apple juice every few hours. (It's also exceptionally good with a splash or two of whisky, if that's your thing.) I've tried making this cider more quickly, like brewing it for a few hours in a stockpot on the stove. But without exception, it's at its best on day three or four, when the flavours are merging together and settling in for the duration.

Give it time. This might be a few seconds or a minute when the question is asked so you're not rushing to the answer. It may be a few days or even longer. If you're a journaling person, you could do some writing and see what comes out. Attend a retreat and talk it out with others. Go for a walk with this question in mind and let your thoughts about it flow in and out while your feet are moving. And keep coming back to it.

Jon, the accountant who was so impressed with the questions we asked in a Foundations session, took the approach I'd want any accountant doing marketing therapy to take. He came prepared, leaned into the questions, and purposefully set aside space afterwards so he could let these things continue to process, to simmer. One session can feel great, but it's in the consistent sessions over time where you begin to see the change happen in your business.

Writing it down. For me, writing things down—literal pen to paper—is one of the single best ways to start the process of change. I ran a client retreat on a remote island, and one of the exercises we did was to write down who we most want to be and things we could do which would help us lean into that person. I wrote it down that day and didn't look at it again for months. But when I did revisit it about six months later, I could literally see change in my life and in my business. I had made subtle changes which had an impact because I didn't just consider it—I wrote it down.

Giving yourself kindness. It's really frustrating, especially as an accountant, not to have "the answer." You're returning to those tendencies to look for what's right, what's correct. In marketing therapy, in creativity, multiple answers are possible. You can do this marketing action or that one. You can build a new rhythm for a hundred days. You can try what someone else tried and experience a big fail or try something small which has a quick win. If you're not getting anywhere, think about the messages you're giving yourself. Are you saying things like "Why is this not working??" or "I should be further forward by now" or "I'm no good at marketing"? Not only is negative self-talk unhelpful, it's destructive. Remember how we talked about the tendency of people to reinforce stereotypes of accountants by saying how boring that would be, how dull? Don't reinforce that kind of thinking with yourself. Imagine saying something you've said to yourself to a good friend or a fellow business owner: "You should be further forward by now" or "You're no good at marketing." It's horrifying to consider because you'd never do that. You would build up, support, cheer on. You'd tell them, "Hey, don't be so hard on yourself! These things take time. Is there anything I can support you with?" Practice saying those things to yourself too.

Above all, marketing therapy involves questions that presume nothing. Question everything: your clients, your team, your purpose in business, your business model. Even the process of coming up with questions to ask and sitting with them for a while will teach you something. After all, creativity involves curiosity, which then leads to learning.

Care more about what you learn than what you get

Choosing what marketing action you will do or invest in always comes back to what you want to *get* from it. And that makes sense. You want marketing which gets a return, which proves, by the numbers, it worked and so you can do more of it. But to figure out what works *for you* and for your firm (which may not be the same as what works for everyone else), you'll need to try things for a while and focus more on what you *learn* than what you get. It's the true heart of creativity: creating simply for the sake of doing it rather than for the return you'll get immediately.

When I successfully completed a 100-day video challenge, I was so proud. I'd tried the challenge multiple times before and not completed it fully. The first time, I did a few videos, and then things trailed off. The second time, I didn't record a video every day, but I stuck at it and had about sixty videos by the end. But this third time, I recorded and published a video on Instagram every single day for one hundred days, and I was so proud of myself. My goal was simply to do it and see what happens, but I also wanted to get more comfortable with video, more familiar. To lean into it quicker. When I shared about it on LinkedIn, an accountant I didn't know commented with the question, "But what was the financial ROI?" I was suddenly tempted to think, *Oh no . . . what a fail. I'm not sure if I can point to a specific client who decided to work with us because of these videos. Did I waste all my time?*

I knew I hadn't because my goal wasn't to record one hundred videos and track the direct cash which flowed into my business from each one. If that was my goal, I would have recorded different kinds of videos, and there's still no guarantee it would have delivered a certain financial result. But my purpose was to learn, to improve, to get better, and all of that I achieved. Later I would look at videos I'd recorded and see a connection to people who bought the DIY video course for *The Accountant Marketer* or a copy of the book itself. Some of those people later enquired about working with me through my creative agency, signed proposals, and worked with us on their brand or website or marketing campaigns. On average, one accounting client spends £48,500 (approximately $65,000) with our agency over a period of two years. Did my one hundred videos contribute to that? Absolutely. Exactly how much? No one knows. What was important in the beginning was that I had challenged myself to creativity, and that's a challenge you always win.

Think about something you tried in the early days of your business. Actually stop for a moment and hark back to those days. Imagine yourself sitting where you used to work—your old office, the home you used to live in, the coffee shop you were working from. For me, it was the second bedroom of a small flat, and it had a window looking out to the car park. I could see the postie coming by on his rounds, neighbours walking their dogs, people coming and going. Get that really clear in your mind. Now think about something you did for your business which you were really excited about. This was going to be the Next Best Thing. It was going to revolutionise your business and probably even your life. What was it?

One of the things I tried was a product called Business Builder Webinars. The idea was to help accountants deliver webinars to their clients on business development topics like marketing or business models or sales. We got guest speakers to record the webinars, and the accountant paid a monthly fee to have these webinars recorded, set up, delivered as live, and (hopefully) attended by their clients and prospects. It was a lead generation opportunity, and it would all tick over automatically without the accountant having to do anything but gather in the leads.

It worked, and it didn't. When I think about the sheer number of hours I and other members of the team spent building this product, it's almost shocking (especially when you compare it to the sales we made from it, which were not exactly significant.) But I believed in this product, and I believed it would help accountants to help their clients, so it felt worth it. Over time, though, we discovered there were foundational areas which needed to be addressed first in order for a project like this to be useful. In order for it to work, they needed a good website, an email marketing system, and an organised and segmented database. Even when they had these things, there could be other foundational elements they needed, like a good brand and a clear brand voice. They might even need to rebrand or change their firm name because the current one was doing damage to the business growth mindset they were trying to portray with these webinars. Ultimately, the accountants were struggling to see the numbers on these webinars because they were missing the foundational components required to make them successful.

The product wasn't a fail. We helped accountants, we helped their clients, and we figured out what areas needed to be reviewed and dealt with before launching something of this magnitude. We got some sales and some revenue from this product, but I got something far more powerful: a learning about how much time to put into a major, significant project before testing it to make sure it really works. I learned that it's fun and exciting to stay up late for weeks on end building the Greatest New Product to Ever Be Revealed of All Time, but if said product isn't quite what people need, it might have been wiser to set up the webinars manually and run them for two or three accountants first. *Then,* if it built traction, turn it into a product and promote it and sell lots of them. I had bought into the repeatable business concept, as if creating something and letting it run is easy. It's not easy. It's bloody hard work. Anyone who has a successful, repeating, recurring product which seems to tick away with no effort has usually put in a hell of a lot of effort in the early days, and they've probably done that ten or twelve times with other products which never resulted in anything. They just don't talk about those fails.

Creativity Exercise

What was your Greatest Idea Ever which failed in some spectacular way? Sit and think about it for a few minutes and make some notes: What was good about it? What didn't work? Think about whether there's something from this you can use to improve an existing project or idea.

The learnings matter. I don't regret what we worked on. But equally, when we come up with a brilliant new idea these days, I pause to think about what the minimum viable product is first. What's the MVP? Is it a document with a video I send to a few clients? Is it a blog post describing a new opportunity? Could I get more by personally emailing or messaging fifteen clients and asking for their opinion? I do that first, and then if things pick up, I can do more and turn it into something.

Summoning help when you're stuck involves your community, your rhythms, and some marketing therapy. It may also mean calling on the machines.

HELP FROM THE MACHINES

You've probably seen *The Terminator*. You know what happens when we let the machines in. They take on a consciousness of their own and, naturally, decide to destroy the human race. Insert eye-roll emoji here for this being the inevitable plot for any future-based film including machines or aliens. Of course they'd always choose violence and war and destruction. None of them would be creative beings, wanting to involve and invite and make better.

As I write this, AI and tools like ChatGPT (which, as one developer said to me, literally *sounds* like it was named by a developer) are in use and taking off at lightning-fast speeds. ChatGPT got to one million users in five days—a feat which took Netflix three and a half years and Instagram two and a half months. It reached *one hundred million* monthly users in two months, and this took Instagram thirty months and TikTok nine months. Of course, by the time you're reading this, even ChatGPT could be the dated version and there are several other, better options. Whatever we thought we knew about speed of adoption is still being broken. Like automated email software and social media scheduling tools and blog topic generators, it can help you and inspire you and, yes, speed things up. It can also be used as a way to avoid really digging into who you truly are—you personally, your firm, your team, the clients you serve—in a rush to "generate content."

For the purposes of simplicity, I'll combine it under one term, AI, but this will refer to anything closely resembling machine intelligence. I expect anything I say about its capabilities will be changed by the time you read it, but it's clear this is an adaptation to the way we do life and work and business. It's like when we got the internet. Yes, it took years to reach the point at which few of us could live our lives without it, but it also took time to move into every area of our lives. I still remember my parents worrying about using online banking. I told them, "Well, by this point, literally everything else in my life is online too, so if online banking is a problem, then everything is a problem." I stopped keeping paper copies of statements or invoices. I got rid of filing boxes. It slowly happened, day by day, and the same thing happened with voice technology and completing payments on your phone rather than by physical card. I still pick up pennies or coins when I find them on my daily walks, but they don't get much use. We'll be using AI so seamlessly we may not fully notice when it has fully changed our lives, our content creation, and our marketing.

With each of these technological changes, there are voices of enthusiasm and voices of panic. There are those gleefully proclaiming, "Yes, this will change everything!" and those groaning, "Oh no, this will change everything!" A few parents use AI to help create custom stories to read to their children at bedtime, and suddenly we're asking, "What does this mean for the future of children's books?" An accountant uses AI to write emails and blog posts, and content writers wonder, "What if this puts content writers out of business?"

AI will—and already has—impacted the creative industry I'm in. We have a team of content writers and designers, and the way they do their work already involves AI and will incorporate more as time goes on. We've even created a PF Strategic Marketing GPT ourselves, based on fourteen years of supporting accountants with their marketing. It includes our methodology and approach as well as the entire contents of my first book *The Accountant Marketer*, and all our resources, briefs, templates, checklists, and support so you can get more strategic help with your marketing as an accountant. (You're welcome to access it free at wearepf.com/gpt.)

As with all technology, there's a human element, and there's a machine element. The question for you is where and how you use each. We'll all be using it more and more in our personal lives, our creative lives, our business lives. How we use it reflects our creativity and our humanity. Right now, content writers aren't in any danger of being replaced by AI; what it does replace is shitty content writers, those whose content isn't original, isn't human, and sounds generic and like everyone else. But it's learning fast, and already authors are using AI to create searchable databases of their own content, and creating

AI versions of themselves, which puts it in a different category altogether.

There's still value in thinking for yourself. It can be really frustrating to spend hours working on a blog post structure, then try it with ChatGPT and realise it's come to very similar conclusions as you did. It's incredible what kind of imagery design AI is already capable of. We could look at all of these capabilities as something to replace us as humans, or we can look at them as an opportunity to draw out the creativity we know we have but struggle sometimes to find or to lean into. This could be one of the best things for your creativity that has ever existed. You need your creative mind to think strategically. Plan how you'll use the resulting content or design or idea. Consider the audience and purpose and what action you want them to take. All this creativity can literally be plugged into the AI tool you're using to bring out—sometimes much faster—what was already there in your mind to begin with.

Right now, prompts are the key. The better your prompt to ChatGPT, the better the outcome. If I type in "write a paragraph for a book on creativity about how AI is shaping the future of creative work," I get something bland and formal sounding which talks about the ever-evolving landscape of creativity and unprecedented opportunities for creative professionals and augmenting human ingenuity with AI's data-driven insights. It hasn't really said very much because it's simply compiling other content. But the more specific the prompt, the better the results are, and you might just have something interesting to read. I'm still playing with it and using it as an idea generator or a support when I'm stuck, but at the moment, I've written every paragraph and every chapter of this book with my own two hands.

As you use AI-related tools (and you will, more and more), all that you're learning about your own personal creativity will help you use it better and get better results from it. Believing you aren't creative and the machines are will only deliver machine-sounding work. But when you approach AI with a recognition of your own creative mindset, with your problem-solving questions and your curious mindset, you will get far more (and faster) than you ever imagined. Let's look at some creative principles to apply to the machine support you use.

Use it to improve, not create. The point is not to rush to generate a bunch of words. Consider the message you most need to share and to whom, and use AI to make that message better. If you have absolutely no idea what to try in marketing, asking ChatGPT will give you generic points you probably knew anyway. But if you have a specific blog post idea based on a question a client or prospect has asked, you can use AI to expand on what you have and help make your own ideas better. If you're stuck on copy for an ads headline or a punchy social media statement, you can get help turning your ideas into more focused messaging. "Give me three subject lines for an email about a new service" is going to produce some really generic subject lines (which are very likely click-baity) because you haven't given ChatGPT much to work with. Instead, you can try a more specific direction. "We are launching a new payroll service for creative agency owners so they don't have to spend time on payroll anymore. Give me three subject lines for an email to these owners about it." Then keep going. Keep saying, "Try it again" or "Like that, but less formal." Whatever it gives you, try another prompt and another until you think, *Oooh, there it is!* You'll still want to spend time on making sure the tone of voice is truly yours (not just clever in an abstract sense) because this is coming from you, not a machine. You can also use AI to help you try out different adaptations to tone of voice. Try making it more formal. Less formal. More friendly. Write it for millennials. You could ask it to write in the style of Shakespeare, of Captain America, of Taylor Swift. Have some fun with it!

Have an opinion. Even in the early days of encouraging accountants to be involved in content creation, I was faced with the question of "Why bother?" Wasn't there already enough content available? Why write a blog post on the pitfalls of doing your own bookkeeping when hundreds, if not thousands, of other accounting or bookkeeping firms have done the same? Yes, they have, but sharing content for your accounting firm isn't solely about providing bland, dry information. It's about providing information together with your style. Your voice. Your opinion. After all, thousands of other accounting firms also have onboarding processes. They may even serve the kind of clients you serve, and do tax returns and management accounts and payroll for those clients. But how do *you* do it? What kinds of things make you *you*? And how do you get that across in your marketing so the buyer (who, remember, makes 70 percent of their buying decision before they ever get in touch) is made aware of it and feels it and begins to have some of their doubts and fears allayed?

Whether you wrote the content all on your own or had help from AI, you want the reader to not only receive the information they're looking for but to also *feel* who you are. Weave your opinion and style and tone into this factual information being shared. This helps the buyer feel a little more confident and less nervous about getting in touch. When they do get in touch, every interaction confirms that all the marketing you've done is for real. All the things you've mentioned aren't just sales speak—they happen. The team members you mention are real humans, not stock photos.

Build out ideas and structure. Using the blog post example mentioned above, you could identify a topic and some key points and create a messy draft—what Brené Brown calls the SFD, the Shitty First Draft. Part of writing a great blog post is not simply getting a few points across but creating headings and subheadings that tell a story and helping the reader grasp it quickly. Use AI to create subheadings that include the keywords you need, then read through all the subheadings together to see if they make sense, have the same style and tense, and help the reader grasp the point more quickly.

Beat writer's block. The single best way I find to beat writer's block is to open the document I'm working on, put my hands to the keyboard, and start typing. Sometimes it's a cobbled-together mess, and I don't even know what I'm saying. There are days I write a thousand words and then read them back the next day and think, *Well, those aren't making it into the final manuscript, that's for sure.* But the point is to keep going. Use AI tools to prompt, support, get started, keep going. Move past the hesitation or fear that this is too big of a project or will take too much effort and just get started.

Use it to proof and edit. Once you have the topic, the rough structure, the bullet points and notes, the headings and subheadings, you can use AI to pull it together and make it make sense. Proof it not only for spelling and grammar but also for flow. Ask it to move paragraphs around, change the order, try it in a different style.

Above all, ask yourself: Are you using AI to avoid work or original thought, or are you using it to enhance your own creativity? To be fair, we might be thinking, *When it comes to it, is there any such thing as original thought?* I still believe there is. You, as a human, are unique, and so am I. Your tone, your opinion, your approach to something make it yours. There's going to be some trial and error, some adjustments and edits and even a few failures along the way. And because of that, remind yourself that you always have permission to reset or restart.

SECTION SIX:

Keeping going

6 KEEPING GOING

PERMISSION TO RESET/RESTART

Pivot without mercy or guilt

If you consider your marketing in terms of pure success or failure, you'll get frustrated. When it comes to creative thinking and marketing, you're not seeking what is right or what is wrong—you're playing with things. Trying. Moving this way and then that way. Changing direction. Yes, you're still checking to see whether it's having an impact or if you are getting what you want and need, but there's room to pivot. Be willing to change your mind. To pivot.

When it comes to creative thinking and marketing, you're not seeking what is right or what is wrong.

This doesn't mean you randomly *squirrel!* all over the place—that tends to happen when you're distracted and don't even have a direction at all. Pivoting means you've been going one direction for a while, and based on the outcomes and your future intentions, you want to turn yourself (or your company or marketing actions) in a slightly different direction using the lessons you learned as your reasons for the turn. Your former actions become the justification for the turning point. It's incremental. Still the same direction but with a shift.

I remember working with an accountant who served clients in a few creative niches: writers, photographers, and editors. As time went on, he noticed more and more photographers were getting in touch. He enjoyed working with them and was signing up a few of them a month or even every week. Instead of turning his entire business towards photographers only, he began to pivot, just a little, to focus content on photographers. He exhibited at several conferences where photographers attended. He wrote guides and recorded video. The firm was still working with writers and editors and other creatives, but he focused his content a little more in the photographer arena.

If you've done something similar, this point is when you may begin to pause and question yourself. Is this a good idea? What if photographers seem to be a good audience, but it turns out later they're not the best clients? How long will this last? What if they all sign up but none end up staying clients? *What if what if what if . . .*

And then you become racked with guilt. Or you want to have mercy on every other creative or business or person who may want to work with you, so you don't pivot at all. You don't change. You just carry on. And you get what you've always been getting.

If a pivot opportunity appears, go ahead with the pivot. Don't let the good quality of mercy become a lack of boundaries as you try to serve everybody. Serving everybody means it's more confusing. Equally, don't let guilt and fear prevent you from a little change which could have a big impact. Pivot now in this small way because you can make another small one later. And another and another. The point of a pivot is to help you *learn.*

The accountant who pivoted to photographers ended up letting go of that pivot and turning his attention entirely to writers. He now works exclusively with writers, which means he's known as the accountant to go to for writers. The photography audience was good for a while, but they weren't who he most enjoyed working with, and they weren't as profitable as his writer audience. He picked what he knew he was good at and what would serve him and the business and kept his focus there. The pivot was useful because of what he learned.

Most of us—and especially accountants—pivot slowly, gradually. If you're walking along a main path, your pivot may look more like a glance to the left, taking a path only slightly off the main one, not suddenly jumping in a plane and flying to another country. Chris Jones, owner of Westbound HQ, exclusively serves the trucking industry. When he told me about his career and the various paths that led to the firm he has now, it was full of slight pivots of this kind. He worked designing wastewater treatment plants, then converting methane to diesel fuel, then selling a lubricant oil product, then breaking into the trucking industry, then buying a franchise in the tax industry. "Some of my pivots weren't intentional," Chris said. "But I took what came to me, and when I got overwhelmed with that, I pivoted again." When he took on a whole bank of clients, he discovered many of them weren't the right kind of clients for his firm, and they spent a full two years weeding those people out. As they focused more on the right kind of client, Chris began to realise they didn't have to be the ones to say no; the prospect would find the pricing too high or get annoyed at the processes and would go elsewhere.

"Our marketing was doing the dividing for us, saying no for us."

Best of all, he's now realising the perfect client is rather elusive; not long after you have perfectly defined the ideal client for your firm, you'll discover your firm is shifting and changing, too, which means the ideal client description changes again. That's normal. Businesses keep changing throughout their entire lives. Sometimes it's a slight shift, like the gentle pivots Chris was taking, and other times, it's more dramatic.

From time to time, you'll pivot so much you've gotten a bit lost, and you'll need to reset and start over. That's part of failure and learning, and that's okay too. Let's look at the concept of a reset.

The reset: You can stop and restart

When it comes to creativity, you're not stuck with what you've decided to work on. If you've tried something and it's not working—the project is beyond your skills, the new niche you pivoted to is not bringing in any clients—you have permission to stop, wipe the slate clean, and try again.

The reset is a conscious decision. Too often, we simply carry on with something we're doing because it's there. Perhaps you've been serving construction businesses for years. Maybe your father who owned the firm before you always served these kinds of businesses and really enjoyed it. You have permission to decide not to work with those anymore. Or it could be pricing. You've always charged this much for tax returns or that much for your monthly bookkeeping clients. Maybe you increased the price a little over the years, but you feel like you couldn't possibly make a big pricing change. It would be too much. They'd say no. You'd lose clients.

When you begin to feel trapped by your former decisions or someone else's decisions affecting you, it may be time for a reset. This means you stop, you review the situation, you gather your information, you make a clear decision, and only then do you start again in the new direction. It's considered and focused; you're not at the whim of whatever happened in the past or the opportunities which came your way that morning. You're the master of your fate, the captain of your soul.

It's fascinating how we can be a leader in one way—running a business, leading a team, bringing on clients, deciding on services—and, in another, feel like we are at the mercy of the fates. Those leadership qualities you already have can be applied to this situation or decision that is trapping you.

So first, you stop. Take a day or a week to stop doing this thing which is weighing on you. This gives you an opportunity to see more clearly. When you're in the weeds, pushing through day by day, doing the next thing and the next thing almost without thought, you're not getting any creative space. Stopping is the first step towards a reset, and it's that simple. You just stop, and you see what happens. It's best if you can choose to stop by your own decision because it's clearer and easier, but far more often the stop is forced on you by illness or family circumstance or the world coming to a screeching halt (like we saw in 2020). This is usually because you're too exhausted to stop, and when you're exhausted or burnt out, you aren't thinking straight. So your body makes the decision for you, and you get sick. Or someone you care about goes into hospital, and you realise how little this other thing you were doing matters. Having life circumstances point out to you that it's time for something to stop is perfectly normal, by the way. We all need it to happen. Often, we've been mulling it over in the back of our minds, and the stop in our life has brought it to the fore.

Creativity Exercise

Pick a project you are really keen on but doesn't seem to be getting much traction. Stop doing anything related to it for a full week. Every time you think of it, turn your attention to something else. Literally ignore it. At the end of the week, put all your attention back on it for an hour. What do you see now that is different?

Remember my story of the photography workshop I went to in Italy and how I thought it would revolutionise my photography business? Instead, I ended up lying on the cold tiles of a floor in an Italian villa, thinking, *I can't go on like this.* So I stopped. As a wedding photographer, this didn't mean stopping all wedding photography instantly. I had weddings booked eighteen months out, and I didn't feel right about cancelling those. So I kept those commitments, but stopping meant I said no to every new photography enquiry that came in.

That was hard. I remember thinking, *What if this is a bad idea? What if I really do want to do wedding photography and lean into it? What if I'm shooting myself in the foot?* And at the same time, I had a curious sense of relief. I put together a templated reply for everyone who messaged or emailed me about their wedding, explaining I wasn't taking on any new weddings for the next year. Whilst many people were disappointed, they were also understanding. It even became refreshing to say no because I was setting the stage in a way which allowed me to actually move about on it. My stage had become so crowded I couldn't move creatively; I was stuck, hemmed in. Now it was opening up, and I had room to breathe. That's a big reason to simply stop—it gives you breathing room so you can think clearly. And this means you can review the situation properly, which is the next stage in your reset.

There's a scene in the film *The Hobbit: The Desolation of Smaug* where Bilbo and the dwarves are walking through a murky forest and everything is dark, misty, and confusing. They're supposed to be staying on the path, but the path is hard to see. There's no light, and there are no open spaces. While they're all arguing and quite literally going round in circles, Bilbo climbs a very tall tree to see if he can pinpoint where they are and where they need to go. When he gets to the top of the tree, out of the confusing webs of the forest, and lifts his head above it into the fresh air, everything is much clearer. He can see how far they've come and where they need to go. He can see the path. Most of all, his head is clear of cobwebs and confusion.

Reviewing the situation is like climbing the tree. Stopping is the first step because you need that miniature shock to the system to help you take it seriously. Once you've stopped (and this may be days or even months after the stop) you can climb the tree, so to speak, and see the big picture. This might mean thinking about or even documenting what was working and what wasn't, sort of an after-the-fact pros and cons list. When I was considering how or whether to move forward with wedding photography, I did a lot of this kind of thinking. *I love capturing that right moment*, I'd think. I loved being able to share the final images with the bride and groom and see them go wild with delight or share their photographs with friends and family and remember again the joy of their day. I loved the challenge of photo editing and the creative aspect of designing the wedding album pages. But on the other hand, I remembered the hard things. Starting at six or seven in the morning and being quite literally on my feet with a heavy bag of camera equipment until nearly midnight. Coming home and being almost guaranteed to get a migraine either that night or the next morning from the activity and lack of water and food. Being exhausted for the next few days while I recovered.

Instantly feeling the pressure to hurry, hurry, hurry with the wedding photos. Questions always poured in quickly: *When will they be ready? Do you have a few we can share now? What about the album? We want to get that as soon as we can!* The clearer my head became with fewer weddings to shoot and more space for thinking, the better I was able to see the cons were starting to outweigh the pros.

Another thing you can do to review the situation is to look ahead. If you keep on doing this thing for the next year or five years or ten years, what will it look like? What will you look like? When I looked ahead with weddings, I saw myself getting more tired, finding it harder and harder to balance both businesses. I also recognised the last few weddings had ceased to feel shiny and new and instead felt like . . . every other wedding. No matter how hard I fought it and reminded myself every wedding was unique and every couple had their own style, there were things I could guarantee would happen, and it often took a lot of energy to deal with those. When I turned my view towards the marketing agency, I could already see the potential of scaling. We'd started to hire a few team members at that point, and they were taking things on to release my time and help me focus in the areas I most wanted to. So when I looked ahead at both paths, I had one which would take more and more from me over time and one which would give back more and more over time. This helped reassure me that my decision to stop temporarily was the right one and helped me think clearly enough to gather my information.

Gathering information may very well be your favourite part of this exercise. This is where you get to look at the numbers and the data. The speed at which you go through these stages is your decision, and it depends on the situation you're in. You might stop, review, and gather information all in the space of an hour or a day. For me, it took a few months before I had enough headspace to look logically at the numbers. How many hours was I spending on each wedding? What was I charging, and what profit was I truly making? How many weddings a year was I getting? How much more work would I need to do to book more weddings? What would I need to charge if I wanted to continue? As we know, the numbers don't lie. Previously, I'd been telling myself it didn't matter if I spent a little extra time with the wedding couple before the big day because it helped improve the quality of the wedding day photographs. I was more comfortable with them and them with me. That was all true; the resulting images were always better when I did a pre-wedding shoot. But when I added up the numbers, from pre-wedding shoot to wedding day to edited images to album, I was spending between seventy-five and ninety hours per wedding. That wasn't counting the time cost of the hours and days I *wasn't* spending working on my marketing agency. So even at the higher end of the fee scale, it really wasn't profitable. Now to be fair to me, I hadn't entered into wedding photography for the money. I did it for the sheer joy of photography and creativity and people, so I hadn't felt too bothered about cold, hard profitability. But now that I'd stopped and reviewed and was looking at the numbers, this information combined with how I felt about it was putting quite a few more ticks in the cons column.

I honestly don't remember the day I made the clear decision to stop doing wedding photography entirely. I continued to say no to new enquiries, and naturally they began to dry up. When I did get a message from a friend who just got engaged, it often started with, *I think I heard you aren't doing weddings anymore, but I thought I'd check . . .* I took my name off the registries and the forums and the places online where I could be found. I closed my Facebook page. I stopped posting on my Instagram account. Then one day, I cancelled the app where I held all the featured wedding photos in albums to display on my wedding photography website, and I set up forwarding so the photography website URL went to my personal website instead. I don't remember what day that was or what motivated me to click that button. I just knew by then every small action I'd been taking during this time on pause was pointing out what my decision already was.

I often use that kind of thinking when I need to make or confirm big decisions in my life. Actions show more about the decision you want to make than words do. All the tiny actions I was taking included slowing down, stopping, deleting, cancelling. None of them showed any interest in reviving, setting up waiting lists, or building content I could use when I restarted everything. So making the clear decision didn't look like me sitting down at my desk with my pros and cons list, looking from one to the other. It meant recognising the decision had already been made, and it was time to accept it.

The final stage, moving on in the new direction, was easy. I was already in that stage and was already moving forward. While all this was going on, I was building more services in the agency, hiring more team members, planning more for the future. I didn't have to pick a new direction because I already had one. Sometimes that's the case, and other times, you do need to pick your new direction once you've finished the last one. Either way, you've had a reset.

This process can happen in literal seconds for something small, like changing from Instagram to LinkedIn for sharing content and connecting with potential clients. It could take a few days, like deciding to stop checking your phone every morning and instead start reading those books piled by your bed or on your office bookshelf. It could take months, like when you stop using one kind of software and set up a new one and begin using that. And it could take a year or more, for things like a life-changing career progression or ending a relationship or selling your business. But whether it takes moments or months, you've still gone through each stage. You stopped, reviewed the situation, gathered your information, made a clear decision, and now you're ready to start again in the new direction.

Once you have that direction, keep going with it.

JUST KEEP GOING

The biggest impact all these principles will have on your life is when you apply them consistently and you just keep going. There's a time to stop, to reset, to change direction, but make that more the rarity than the rule. Whether you're on a roll or see little hints of results or are simply enjoying the process, keep going in the same direction and don't give up.

In my first book, *The Accountant Marketer*, I mentioned the correlation between the process of making Scottish whisky and the process of creating good content. It takes a minimum of three years to be considered whisky, and most distilleries will let their whiskies mature in the cask for ten, fifteen, twenty-five, and even fifty years to get something really beautiful (and profitable!). As with whisky, so, too, with marketing and creativity—the right way is the long way. And it involves doing good work, right down to the detail.

Scottish whisky uses only three ingredients: yeast, barley, and water. There's flexibility available in how those ingredients are combined, how they are distilled, the level of peat smoke used to roast and dry the barley, but every bottle of Scottish whisky comes back to those core three ingredients. As we talked about at the beginning of this book, creativity involves the two simple ingredients of problem-solving and curiosity. The third ingredient is persistence.

You will never get a good bottle of whisky in a hurry. And the maturing process of whisky happens in the dark. For years, the whisky is sitting quietly in barrels, maturing. These barrels are lined up in massive warehouses, stretching row upon row, waiting, letting the flavours and colours of the barrels bring life to the clear distilled liquid. When you look at the change over the years, it's slight every year, but the longer it sits there, the richer and more intense the colours and flavours become. It needs that time before it can be poured out of the barrels and into the bottles to be displayed and sold and tasted and enjoyed. It needs to be tested too; the master distiller will take small samples from the cask as the whisky is maturing and decide whether it's ready or whether it will sit for several more years.

"Keep going" doesn't mean a relentless, unceasing pace. It can be slow and steady. Patient. The point of persistence is that you keep going in the same direction.

"Keep going" doesn't mean a relentless, unceasing pace. It can be slow and steady. Patient. The point of persistence is that you keep going in the same direction.

Some of your creativity will mature in the dark. You'll create a new asset you're really proud of, but only a few clients see it. You work on a structure for the book you want to write or the podcast you want to put out, but it's only shared with your business partner or a few members of the marketing team. That's okay. When it's ready to come into the light and be bottled and sold, you'll be grateful for that maturing time which has made it better. Stronger.

Like the master distiller, you'll need to edit and adjust your direction slightly as time goes on. Just like when one "expression" of whisky (a specific bottling or version of a particular brand) is moved from one cask to another to enhance the flavour—perhaps from a bourbon cask to an oloroso wine cask—what you've been working on might need to shift too. You've been writing blog posts for years, and now it's time to put them into a PDF guide or even a book. You've been working with one particular type of client for years, and now you have the core structured concepts to build a course for this kind of client. You've written all the content for the course, and now it's time to record videos.

Part of keeping going means figuring out what to keep and what to let go. Sometimes a master distiller will taste a whisky to see how it's getting on as it matures, only to discover it has an acidic, vinegar taste. When that happens, the whole barrel has to be thrown out. There's no saving it. Some of what you've been working on will not apply anymore. It's not relevant, not needed, not reflective of your changing brand. That's okay. Let it go. Keep creating, keep tasting, and when it gets acidic, let it go.

One of the challenges to keeping going is finding the balance between what you love to do and what others need. Not everyone likes every kind of whisky. Some people don't like any kind. That's okay. One of my favourite whisky distillery tours is the one at Tobermory Distillery on the Isle of Mull. The first time I did the tour, there was a tasting session at the end. This distillery produces both a peated (smoky) and unpeated whisky, so you have multiple options to taste. Some people liked the lighter, unpeated expression; some preferred the stronger, smokier version. Some put a few drops of water into their whisky. Some wanted it with ice. Some didn't like any version of it at all. The tour guide said, "The best way to drink whisky is the way you want to drink it." Despite what some connoisseurs may try to tell you, there isn't a right way or a wrong way to drink whisky. There's the way you enjoy it. It's made to be enjoyed.

Creativity is meant to bring out the best of you, and it's

meant to be enjoyed. You may love writing or really struggle to put a hundred words together. You may find recording videos easy, or you may avoid it like the plague. You may enjoy puzzles or starting new businesses or decorating homes or building websites. Once you find your lane, stay in it, and keep going in the same direction. Not everyone will care about what you're creating and how you're doing it. That's okay. You keep going. Remember, their preferences don't reflect on your identity. You make your choices and let them make theirs.

After all, preferences can change over time. I've lost count of the number of people who have visited me in Scotland and said, "Oh, I don't like whisky." Nine times out of ten when I ask what they don't like about it, they either tried to drink it like a shot (Pro tip: Please, for the love of all things holy, don't do *shots* of Scottish single malt whisky), or they've only tried cheap or blended whiskies which tasted acidic and harsh. I remember driving some friends from America into the Scottish Highlands and around the Isle of Skye, and we had multiple conversations about whisky as we made our way up and down the winding roads. One of them said she didn't think she liked whisky but admitted she'd never really tried any. She thought it was meant to be chugged quickly, which didn't appeal to her. One night at dinner, we were near Ben Nevis, and I ordered a dram of a Ben Nevis whisky I knew to be quite light, not too peaty or intense. I asked if she wanted to try some. She took a small sip, thought about it, and her face brightened with interest. "Now that," she said, "I could come to like!" A few nights later, I was drinking a darker, smokier, more intense whisky from the Isle of Skye's Talisker distillery, and even the slight whiff she had of my glass was enough. "No, I don't think I'll try that one," she said. "But if we could find the other one I had the other night, I might buy a bottle!" To each their own enjoyment, but you (or others) may need to try a variety of things first before you confirm whether you like it or not.

And even if you enjoy it, even if you're making good progress, you will be tempted to give up at some point. For me, it's when I get near the finish line.

Self-sabotage: The temptation to give up near the finish line

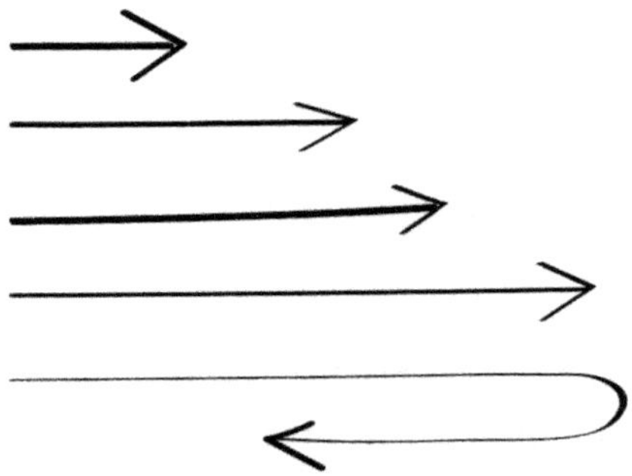

This image is me. In every major achievement in my life, I've gotten cold feet or slowed down or hesitated or got sick or *something* right before the end. Depending on how significant the achievement is, it might be a day or a week before I get there, or it might be a few months. I've seen this in making healthier choices for my body, in moving house, and in every book I write. When I was writing my first book, I hadn't intended *that* to be the first one. I had other books I wanted to write, like this one! There were other topics I thought were more interesting and more fun with more creativity, sketching, and clever ways to lay out the book. But I opened a document to make notes of the key points about the Accelerator group I was running to share with the team as they helped me co-lead it. Then I started pulling content from blogs I'd been writing for the previous ten years, then decided to turn it into a guide, and when I counted the words, I realised I had a book. And then I sort of shut down. I set it aside, almost in a panic, and wasn't sure what to do or how to move it from the document to a published book. It took me months to pick it back up and get editing and developmental and publishing support, and ultimately it was three years from start to finish to get it published.

I listened to a podcast called *The Place We Find Ourselves* which explained how the nervous system is constantly surveying your environment to determine how safe and supported you feel. Based on that level of safety or lack thereof (or anything that feels remotely threatening), the system triggers reactions of how to respond, including the fight, flight, or freeze options, as well as the complete shutdown. Fight or flight you're familiar with. The freeze option means you're extra aware, fully on alert, ready to take another action but not moving at all. The shutdown option means you're blank. Not moving. Given up. Nothing is going to help, so you just stop.

> *More often than we care to admit, we don't get what we want because we quit early or we didn't take the necessary risk to get it.*
> —*Matthew McConaughey,* Greenlights

This is what my brain does to me when I get too close to an impossible goal or a goal that is tough and someone told me I could never do it. Maybe no one told me that—maybe it was my own brain telling me that. Maybe I was the one saying, "You can never do it," and then I showed myself, and now the two me's are in conflict and I don't know how to decide which one wins. So I just freeze and do nothing, stuck in an endless state of paralysis.

This may not be your problem. You might hit the shutdown earlier or not at all. But for those of us who get close to a goal and either shut down completely or go on pause and find it hard to hit the start button, addressing self-sabotage is part of keeping going. Not giving up. Seeing it through all the way to the end.

I thought about some of the goals I achieved when I didn't go through as much (or any) self-sabotage. In the early days of my marketing agency, I had someone tell me I would not make it a success. This wasn't even a keyboard warrior; this was someone who had known me for years saying it right to my face. I wouldn't be able to manage it, they said, especially the financial element. I'd fail. It was harsh to hear, especially when I knew deep down it wasn't true, but I pressed on anyway. I got a loan I needed, I got good accountants to advise me and help me along the way, and I carried on. Paying off the loan was a big deal, a goal connected to making PF a success, and yet as I got close to the end, I sort of forgot about the original goal of paying off the debt. I stayed focused on my own goal of having a profitable, scalable agency in which my team were doing the client work and I was doing the strategy and the leadership and being the caretaker of the culture. I tracked it and watched how far I'd come and some days bemoaned how long it was taking . . . and suddenly one December, I realised I had one more payment before the loan would be fully paid off. A month later, I made the last payment and was free.

There are a few reasons I saw that one through to the end without self-sabotage. First, the goal itself comprised multiple goals in one, so I was able to focus on the more important element of building a scalable business rather than simply paying off the loan. This meant the original goal was still there, still being worked towards, but it wasn't consuming me. There were other things to think about. The second reason was the series of small steps done on a daily (or, in this case, monthly) basis which became habit. The loan payment was set up and went out every month. We accounted for it in the finances, but it just happened month after month in the background while I paid attention to the people and the processes and our services. There's less opportunity for self-sabotage when the goal is broken down into small steps or small payments which happen automatically.

There's another way to deal with self-sabotage, and that's to literally trick your mind. What I find hilarious about this approach is you and your mind know exactly what's going on. There's really no trick because everyone's in on it. Let me give you an example. I lived in a flat for ten years with no dishwasher. Doing dishes was one of those tasks which really wasn't a big deal, but it *became* a big deal in my mind, and I'd avoid it until it became something I had to tackle, and then it was even harder. Thinking about hand-washing all of those dishes got discouraging. So instead, I'd trick my mind by saying, "Listen. I'm not going to wash *all* the dishes. All I'm going to do is fill the sink with hot soapy water. That's it." But once I did that and stood there with a sink full of hot soapy water, I'd figure I may as well wash a dish or two . . . and before I knew it, they were all done.

Even while saying that to myself I knew—I *knew*—I'd end up washing every single dish and feel very proud and relieved as I stood in my shining kitchen. But I had to approach it differently. You may need to approach a project or building a creative mindset or setting a creative rhythm with a bit of a trick. What's amazing is the fact you'll know it's a trick when you start and it still works.

The alternative, self-sabotage, is frustrating and even angering. It's confusing to see myself so close to a goal and then I slow down or even stop when I could push that little bit more and be there. There are many reasons for our self-sabotage, and yours will be different than mine. Maybe you get fearful of what it looks like to arrive. Maybe you doubt your own abilities. Maybe you are your own worst critic when everyone else is saying, "You can do it," believing in you more than you are yourself. Maybe there's a part of you saying, *You're not that good. Don't pretend to be someone you're not.*

When we get there, when we arrive at our goal, other goals appear or are in progress. So the opportunity for self-sabotage never ends. I wonder if it's the struggle of the creative mind: We fight to create and to do good, and when it seems we may be achieving, we become our worst enemy and turn on ourselves.

I haven't eradicated self-sabotage in my life. But there are a few approaches, a few wonderings, which help me as I continue to deal with it and may help you too. We've looked at breaking the goal down into habitual, recurring tasks that happen without effort and the goal is achieved before you know it. Tricking your mind follows a similar approach; it's like you're saying to yourself, *The goal doesn't matter anymore. All that matters is this one next thing.* Once that thing is done, you do the next apparent thing, and before you know it, the goal is reached.

Another one that helps is having a deadline to meet. I've always achieved more closer to a deadline than before it; the pressure of needing to finish helps me finish. This must be a real deadline with consequences of some kind if it's not met. When my publisher sets dates for editing and reviewing one of my books, I know we have some flexibility. At the same time, I need to treat these deadlines as real, or else I'll keep moving them endlessly and we won't achieve the goal (a published book). When we set a date for pre-order and for publication, I start telling people about it. I know that if I don't do the tasks to get us towards those dates, the deadlines will have to be moved, which means I'll need to tell everyone, "Yes, we said it would be ready on this date, but it's not yet, and we had to move the date." The more people you tell, the more public you are about your deadline, the more motivating it becomes. You'll know this in your accounting firm; you and your clients deal with deadlines every day. The tax return or the company accounts must be submitted by this particular date. If not, there are penalties to pay. Interest. Consequences. Yes, there are extensions and ways to move the deadline if you need to, but the deadline looms over all and motivates everyone to do their part so the deadline is met.

It's not merely one deadline either. Sometimes you've got to create multiple deadlines to reach the one everyone knows about. One of the challenges for accountants sharing a tax return deadline, for instance, is that everyone knows the ultimate deadline date—the thirty-first of January in the UK and the fifteenth of April in the States. But to reach that deadline, things need to be submitted long before that. Drafts created and reviewed. Edits made. Returns signed. So if your client comes sailing in on the fourteenth of April, they may believe they've met the deadline, but together you haven't because there isn't enough time for everything else that needs to be done. So you have to re-educate your client. Explain all the steps you and your team follow and how many days this takes and set an earlier deadline, different than the one the government is telling everyone about, the one they're holding in their mind. I know some accountants in the UK who tell their clients they must submit everything on their end by the thirty-first of October the year before to give the firm enough time to complete the return. If it's submitted by the end of November, there's a slight increase to the fee, a small percentage increase (say 5 percent). If it's submitted by the end of December, there's a more significant increase to the fee, say 10 percent. And if it's submitted anytime in January, there's no guarantee the return will be finished on time, so in addition to a hefty fee with a 20 percent increase on the original, there may be penalties and interest to pay as well. These deadlines only work if they're communicated clearly and consistently. You don't want someone showing up mid-January having no idea of the adjusted deadline. Email them and send letters and send texts and share it in your client community group, and make sure everyone knows the consequences of missing a deadline. It keeps you motivated and keeps you on track. Creating or receiving a public deadline is one thing; creating interim deadlines to reach it is another.

Once you've been consistent with the small things, a deadline is more achievable. It's motivational. The song "I See Fire" by Ed Sheeran plays at the end of the third Hobbit film, directed by Peter Jackson. I remember loving the song before I even saw the film. It fit the story so perfectly. I could see the fire in the song. But what was even more impressive to me was the fact that this song was written and recorded in one day. Peter Jackson had written to Ed Sheeran on a Sunday morning, asking if he was interested. Ed would need to fly to New Zealand to watch the (yet unreleased) movie so the song would fit what the audience saw. Forty-eight hours later, Ed was there, watched the film, went into a room, and started working on writing and singing. "Much of what you will hear on this song was recorded that same day," Jackson says, "with a few overdubs and tweaks the following day." Even more amazingly, Jackson recounts, Ed decided he wanted to overdub some violin playing. "Despite having never played the violin in his life, Ed thought he might try overdubbing one himself, and [Peter Jackson's daughter] raced out to borrow a rather battered one from a school friend."

I was blown away. Here is a powerful, beautiful song, appropriate to the film. I'd expect it would take days, if not months, to get it right. Ed would be sitting in a corner, on a plane, at home, in various locations scratching at his lyrics, getting this word right and changing that one. He would watch the film multiple times to make sure he got the feel and also ensure he wasn't missing anything. This is big project stuff.

Instead, Ed hops on a plane, watches the new Hobbit film once, and then goes into a room to start pounding out lyrics and music. He borrows an old violin and plays it himself, having never played the violin before. A few tweaks later, the song is done, it's added to the credits of the film, and now I can listen to it on Spotify anytime I want.

Sometimes when you're considering a big project or wanting to unleash your creative mindset in a particular way, you can get hung up on what you imagine the rules to be. If you're writing a book, it has to take years. Creating and publishing a podcast needs an entire army of creatives to make it good. Delivering a presentation or running an event requires a year of planning. Yes, all of those could happen and do happen. We take our time and create strategies and think it through, and many times that's the best approach. But since marketing is in the creative category, there aren't rules or regulations to follow. You don't have to check in with the HMRC or the IRS and fill in an online form and pay a fee and wait for confirmation before you start posting more on social media. You don't need to hire a ten-person marketing team to craft your email newsletter. Creative tasks can be done in a day. You can fire out something to the best of your ability (which is probably very good) and let it go. Let it happen.

Note that Ed didn't work alone. He had a team of people giving him the bits and pieces he needed (setting him up to watch the film, putting him in a recording studio, racing out to borrow a violin). It wasn't his first time recording a song, and he had a track record of doing it well. But Peter Jackson surrounded him with the right people and tools and told him to go for it, and he did. You, too, could achieve something significant, something creative, in a single day. What might that be for you?

Another way to address self-sabotage is by looking at the big picture. Remind yourself of why you're doing this in the first place. What motivated you to start? What inspired you or kicked off your journey? This might have been seeing others' results and believing this was possible for you too. Go back to those results. You could even combine this with tricking your mind and pretend you're at the beginning again. Why do this? What's it going to deliver? How will it—or might it—help you, your firm, your life? If things have changed since those early days, re-evaluate and readjust.

You also need to reconnect that big picture back to the small steps. Break it down into what's easy and what's small. The entrepreneurial mindset is brilliant at starting things but not always so good at finishing things because finishing is the hard part. You almost have to love the boring. After all, lofty goals and noble ambitions are the easy part. The tough part is waking up at six in the morning after you've only had a few hours' sleep because someone in the household was sick and opening the laptop or going for the run or simply *showing up*. How many times have you seen someone accomplish a goal or launch a new business or write a book and think, *I had that idea! I could have done that.* The difference between your idea and their accomplishment is in the daily, small, even boring tasks repeated over and over.

Let's look at the boring for a moment.

Learn to love the boring

For those of us in a culture driven, focused, even hell-bent on efficiency, we avoid boredom at all costs. Train delayed? Pull out your phone. Not able to sleep at night? Open Netflix.

> *The iPhone is killing our discipline, killing our ability for solitude, and killing our ability to be bored.*
>
> —*James Victore*

Yes, the phone helps us avoid our boredom, but as creative beings who take responsibility for our own creativity and our own results, let's not use phones or technology of any kind to excuse our own decisions. Notifications and Netflix episodes are purposefully crafted to motivate us to click, to open, to continue. Grocery stores are designed to motivate us to buy the snacks, the sugar, the fizzy juice. Homes are designed to keep us comfortable and not to step outside for a walk or to the gym. But even with all of this, we still have choices. When we carefully protect ourselves from ever being bored, we can also be cutting off the oxygen to our creativity. It needs a little room to flow, and boredom can work like an oxygen tube.

Bringing a little boredom into your life is a choice. It's a choice like the one you're making by reading this book: You're recognising your creative mindset, leaning into it, saying, "This is available to me, and I'm going to access it."

The hardest part about embracing boredom for even five minutes is that it's . . . boring. Some of the creative exercises and rhythms we've talked about in this book are compelling or at least intriguing. This one is not—at first, that is. This is one of those exercises you may need to suffer through to get to the good stuff. As you begin to give your brain that creative oxygen, it will (falsely) give you the message that *it is going to die*. Your creative brain has been starved of this oxygen, so it may respond like a small child—with panic and a stubborn digging in of heels and arms grumpily folded, waiting for it to be over. "I don't like this," your brain will say. "I don't live in the 1800s. I have a phone and electricity and a car and literally no reason in the world to be sitting here doing nothing. Stop it."

What's utterly fascinating to me is that in order to release itself from what it believes to be a prison, your mind will then —creatively—come up with solutions for this release. "We could watch a movie, even a documentary! That's not mind-numbing behaviour. We're investing in your knowledge. Or what about going to the gym? You always say you're going to, and now is your chance." The moment you allow yourself to be bored, the creativity will begin. There's nothing at all in the world wrong with watching a film or a documentary or going to the gym. But there are creative outcomes to be plumbed at the depths of your brain, and sometimes only boredom will bring them out.

How do you begin to let boredom in? Yes, it might mean literally sitting on the sofa and staring at the wall, but it doesn't have to only be that. You could sit outside on a bench and stare out at the day. Travel to a beach without all the normal accoutrements of blanket and book and snacks and flask of coffee. Simply sit and watch the waves. Go for a walk or a run without your AirPods in, not listening to music or podcasts but simply being with yourself. The important thing is to put yourself in a place where your mind can wander. If your feet need to wander too, let them. I get most of my good ideas on my daily walk in the nearby woods. The birds are chirping, and the water in the river nearby is flowing, and I can hear my feet hitting the path, one after the other. I've noticed when I'm struggling a little with something, it can feel easy for me to go out on a walk. I know the act of walking quietly on a wooded path will either help me process all the busyness or bring out the ideas which will help me get unstuck. But I've also discovered when I'm *really* struggling, when I feel low or discouraged or everything is too much of a weight, the last thing I want to do is go out a walk. I feel too heavy, mentally and emotionally, to move. So I go outside and sit in my garden and watch the trees move in the wind. Or I watch the little birds who come to hop around and explore this little world of mine.

You'll be tempted to put on music or a podcast or a TV show—resist that temptation. All those are in the category of entertainment, and the word entertainment literally means "diversion." Anything entertaining is there to divert you, to move your mind away from boredom or creativity and let it flow on a different path, a predetermined path. When you're watching Netflix, the show is the one telling you which path your brain will take. When you open your phone and see all those little red notifications, they are the ones directing your path. You've lost control for a moment and given it over to these things. Take your control back, but before you start wielding your power, start by simply letting the dust settle.

You're also going to have to keep it really short at the beginning. Your boredom muscle is going to resist you. After I broke my ankle and the bone healed, it took a long time for the rest of my body to heal too. I thought it would be quick, but I'd forgotten when you stop moving certain muscles, they sort of take the huff a bit. "Fine," they say. "You don't want to use me? I'll give up." Walking was hard, and stairs were a challenge, and I needed my physio exercises every day or my ankle would get stiff again. If you haven't practised boredom much (or at all), start with a minute. Or five minutes. Literally put a timer on your watch or on your phone, and don't look at it for that length of time. Practise one of these boredom exercises and see how long you last. You might even find yourself counting the seconds. How boring.

Here's a list of a few ways you can try letting boredom in.

- Put together a puzzle. Your hands and eyes are busy, but your mind has space to wander. You might even find yourself thinking about things related to the picture you're putting together.
- Go for a walk, perhaps a really boring walk, which goes on for miles in the same direction.
- Take a drive. Again, do it without music or phone calls or fillers—just you and the car and the rolling miles.
- Sit in a chair, or sit outside. If by doing this you are inviting conversation and distraction, find another outside place where the world can swirl

around you: a park, a museum, a coffee shop, the woods.

- Hand-wash dishes or do ironing. Your hands have plenty to do, so your mind has room to roam. Let yourself stand there at the sink staring out the window for a minute. (I'm guessing that's as long as you'll last, at least at first.)
- Take a train journey. It doesn't even have to be for a particular purpose. You could pick a destination, take the train there, and take it back. *How boring*, you think. *That's pointless.* Perfect!
- Go to a restaurant or a coffee shop, order something small you can savour, and sit quietly at the table. Do some people-watching. Notice what's going on around you: the servers, the cooks or baristas, the other diners.

Creativity Exercise

Pick one of the boredom tasks listed here and do that task for thirty minutes (or even ten) without any music, podcasts, or other distractions, ideally without your phone anywhere next to you. After it's done, let it simmer. Don't pressure yourself to get an outcome. Something will come of it, but it may not be straight away.

The outcome of boredom will not be great at first. *What a stupid exercise*, you'll think as you get up in relief after your five-minute timer goes off. *Thanks a lot for that pointless waste of time.* But I can almost guarantee you there will be some outcome from it either later that day or later that week. There will be a thought or an idea which was stirred up. Perhaps you noticed the way someone spoke or worked or the kind of coffee they ordered. You feel bored, but your mind is actually at work. Let it get to work and do things without the typical daily restraints you're continually latching on to it, the handcuffs of the mind that come from your routine, your busyness, your hurry, and your entertainment.

> *She was sitting there waiting for something or somebody and, since sitting and waiting was the only thing to do just then, she sat and waited with all her might and main.*
>
> —Anne of Green Gables

I love this quote about Anne Shirley in this classic book by L. M. Montgomery. I can see her there, sitting on a bench at the train station, holding her carpetbag and waiting "with all her might and main." This is almost the opposite of boredom; she's moved on from boredom and allowed creativity to fill her mind completely. When she's finally picked up by the person she is waiting for, she explains she was imagining all the things which might have prevented him coming and had decided if he never arrived, she would climb the nearby cherry tree and sleep in it all night. If you have to be bored, then, like Anne, be bored with all the power available to you. Let it take you away for a few minutes. You can always come back.

AFTERWORD

You aren't boring. You are creative. And now you have some idea of the creativity already within you—not art but problem-solving and curiosity and persistence. Using these along with daily rhythms and a practise of service design in your business will change the approach you take to marketing and ultimately will change the results you get.

Embracing your creativity as an accountant means recognising you already have all the tools. They're within you. Yes, there are books you can read and exercises and activities you can do, but you're not "making yourself creative." You're leaning into the creativity you already have.

When I was at university all those years ago and people told me accounting was boring, I actually believed it myself for a few years. Or maybe I gave in to peer pressure. Choosing accountancy as my field of study was boring and uncool. I even made up an answer sometimes to avoid the question, telling people I was studying astronomy with a minor in criminal justice.

But one day I was in an accounting class and someone who worked for the FBI came to speak to us. They told us about forensic accounting and their job as an accountant for the FBI and the kind of work they did every day. I remember this person saying, "Getting a degree in accounting doesn't mean you're stuck in a dark corner with one of those banker's lamps." Suddenly, accounting went from being very boring to potentially very cool. There were other examples too. My favourite accounting professor gave us a group project based on the real, live annual accounts of the Pepsi Company. By digging into every corner of those documents, I learned about the other companies and brands owned by Pepsi and the profitability thereof. It all became very real. It turned accounting from something dry and boring into something which integrated with daily life—with *my* daily life.

I didn't end up working for the FBI or for Pepsi. But I did end up running a wedding photography business and setting up a marketing agency and moving from America to Scotland, so my journey from studying accounting and getting my CPA qualification moved far beyond what I and my fellow university students had presumed.

Yours has too. Whether it's choosing a particular audience to work with (such as dentists or interior designers or gamers), changing the way you set up your processes and systems, creating a YouTube channel, writing a book, or building your own website, all of these approaches to your accounting firm involve asking questions. Solving problems. And exploring out of curiosity.

That's creativity.

So what will you do with this newfound creativity or at least this opportunity to examine your mindset? How will you use the creativity you already have?

There are a lot of suggestions in this book. If I had to choose one above all, it would be to start by building a single simple rhythm of some kind of creativity into your life. Rhythms and patterns help take your inner creativity and apply it to what's going on in your life and business every day. Every meeting, every project has potential to become something only *slightly* better because you apply your creative mindset to it. And those slight improvements, day after day, are the ones that turn into the big breakthroughs.

To help you decide what direction to begin with, think about what area is holding you back the most. Or consider an aspect of your business or your life which feels stuck or has slowed down. You can also look at the opportunities of your life, areas you *know* can bring out the best of you if you really apply yourself.

All these patterns you've learned about—how creativity doesn't have to equal art, how it includes failure and is collaborative—can be applied in small ways in those slight improvements, these little rhythms, day after day.

And then keep going!

Stay creative, stay kind, and just keep going.

APPENDIX

Download the Creative Workbook at karenlreyburn.com/creative-workbook.

Creativity Exercises

Section 2: WHY IT MATTERS AND HOW IT IMPACTS YOUR MARKETING

- Pick a different chair in the room you usually work in or move your desk for a different view. Work from there for a day and see what difference it makes to your mindset.
- Pretend you're a new client signing up to work with your accounting firm. Book the meetings, sign the proposal, get the emails, experience the process to the best of your ability. When you notice something that could be confusing or frustrating, fix even one small aspect of that thing. Your next client will be grateful for it—and your systems will slowly improve.

- Identify one big project being held up right now by a significant task or issue. Imagine that issue was suddenly and magically fixed today. What would happen next? This will point you to something you can work on (like content for an email or a video script) today, which you can use once the bigger issue is solved.
- Take ten minutes in your next team meet to ask the team who their absolute favourite client is that week. What happened in the week that caused them to feel like this client was their favourite? What qualities did that client demonstrate with their actions?
- Pick a company you've visited or bought from in the past month that offered a unique experience you were impressed by. Make notes about this: What did they do? When did it happen? What did you expect, and how did this experience make you feel? Then think about something small you can change or try in your firm based on this experience.

Section 3: WHY YOU RESIST IT

- Pick a fail you or your firm has experienced in the past month, something you tried that went either slightly or spectacularly wrong. What is the number one learning you got from that? If you haven't already, share that with your team.
- Pick video, writing, or social media. In that category, create something every day for a month—a short video, a total word count, a social post. At the end of the thirty days, look back and identify one thing you've learned which you can use in your firm's marketing.

- Choose a failure you've been feeling annoyed or even guilty about. Ask yourself these three questions: What went well? What went wrong? And what will I do differently? This simple approach can help focus you on the learning, not the guilt.
- Pick an animal you like (mine would be a puffin). Set a timer for five minutes. Using either pen and paper or a tablet, sketch as many versions of this animal as you can until the timer goes off. Use your phone to give you ideas to sketch from or copy. Then . . . do nothing with the results. Don't post or share them; just consider what you noticed about the process and the result.

Section 4: GETTING STARTED: Finding your rhythm

- Pick a habit you keep trying but failing to implement in your life. Look around at existing habits you are being consistent with. How can you attach this new habit to a tried and true one?
- Think about the last holiday you took where you felt truly rested. Make a list of three things you did while you were rested. How might you do one of these in a small way during one of the working days this week?

Section 5: GETTING HELP

- Choose something you've been working on and have excitement about but haven't shown anyone yet. Share it with your mastermind, marketing community, or a group of like-minded business owners and ask for feedback. Don't feel obliged to implement all their suggestions, but look for patterns of something you might have missed seeing.

- What was your Greatest Idea Ever which failed in some spectacular way? Sit and think about it for a few minutes and make some notes: What was good about it? What didn't work? Think about whether there's something from this you can use to improve an existing project or idea.

Section 6: KEEPING GOING

- Pick a project you are really keen on but doesn't seem to be getting much traction. Stop doing anything related to it for a full week. Every time you think of it, turn your attention to something else. Literally ignore it. At the end of the week, put all your attention back on it for an hour. What do you see now that is different?
- Pick one of the boredom tasks listed here and do that task for thirty minutes (or even ten) without any music, podcasts, or other distractions, ideally without your phone anywhere next to you. After it's done, let it simmer. Don't pressure yourself to get an outcome. Something will come of it, but it may not be straight away.

ACKNOWLEDGMENTS

Creativity is a strange thing. Some days it flows when I'm in the mood, and other days it seems so far away I can never find it again.

Many of us are living through heavy times. Our grandparents might tell us it has been this way before and will be this way again, but for some of us, it was our first time going through a worldwide event like COVID, which impacted us mentally and emotionally more than we knew at the time. Or the *waves hands at everything* world and life as we know it, which doesn't seem to have a name, but weighs heavy and costs more and has a mental and emotional impact on us day after day.

Add to this the ever-present AI, which fills us with (sometimes in rotating order) energy, inspiration, frustration, and cynicism. Perhaps a little like creativity itself!

Whilst writing this book, I spun through all the cycles of creativity, from bursts of motivation to slogs of despair. After finishing the core content, there were periods of time where I did nothing with it. There were also moments when I got a brilliant idea and followed it through and rode the wave for months afterwards. I felt everything you feel when you consider creativity, and even after completing an entire book about it, I'm still unraveling its mysteries.

The people who have been with me along the way, and who show me by example their own forms of creativity and give me hope again, are:

My mum, who is creative in her own unique ways and one

of the most generous people I know. Generosity relieves the mind and revives creativity when it's been low.

My sister Janice, who is always at the other end of the phone—and sometimes the plane—when I need her. Who listens to my moans and laughs with my mistakes and reminds me that it will all be okay in the end. Which it usually is.

My family in the States, who get bursts of time with me and know both the former me and the present me: Pin, DJ, Laura, Audrey, Jude, Jake, Marcus, Luke & Lena and Willow, Zach, Jeb, Scott, Velvet, Marin, Anika & Nikolai.

Jason Staats, who uses his creativity for good in the accounting industry and always surprises me with his instant willingness to support others who are doing good things. Time after time I would think, "He's so important, he won't be able to help with this," and without exception, you'd stop and help. Thanks for stopping to listen, for asking great questions, for leaping into action when needed, and for the remarkable flow of ideas, so many of which get implemented. I still think the only way you get this much done is because you have like seven AI clones all working seamlessly together, but either way, I appreciate you (and the Staats Seven).

The PF team in all its iterations. This company keeps changing with the years, the industry, the client needs, and with me personally. There are so many people who have worked for and with PF who have influenced me in the smallest ways (which has a big impact). Particular thanks to Beccy Pope, who has been a steady support to my creativity and business (and life) for over nine years.

The MAP accounting team, who have been my people since the day I took over PF entirely on my own, and in particular David Arden, who has seen me through some pretty rough days and remained calm and logical so I could keep exercising my wild creativity. As entrepreneurs, our businesses affect our lives directly on a daily basis, so David is literally a business-saver as well as a lifesaver.

Lauren Taylor Shute, Brooke Suermann, and the team at Intrepid Literary. I still haven't found any company who does what you do for authors, and although the process feels slow at times, I see the impact of good, steady publishing work and am grateful that we have completed book two and can move on to books three and four and on and on! I still am amazed that, for me, writing the book is the easy part; it's the editing and publishing and promoting which takes the time.

Ann Handley, author of *Everybody Writes* and *Content Rules* and who literally signed my copy of her book with "now we are best friends," which I hold to like a contract. Our random bursts of WhatsApp messages inspire me and remind me to keep going, and your progress as an author reminds me that it's not always the fastest road, but it's the best one.

My hardworking and incredibly creative friends who share my island home, particularly Donna and Ed, who connect intense creativity to deep needs and wants that people have and create businesses that make life better for so many humans. Their resilience reminds me to keep going and that the combination of creativity and business is a cycle, not a task to complete. (And their sauna provides a much-needed restoration when my creativity is low.)

Our creative clients who talk through their ideas with me and stir up creativity again: Jonathan and Meghan Godwin from Follow the Wolf, Sharon Baker of Kinder, Georgi and Emma from Starfish, Paul Redmond, Lauren Harvey, James Lizars, Andrew McVinish, Jason and Julie of Thriveal/Blumer, Barrett Young of GWCPAs, and so many others whose names are not here but their impact still resonates in my business and personal life. It can be hard to become true friends with people who pay you money for a service because the business part has to come first. I'm eternally grateful for those who are able to make and keep connections, have hard conversations when needed, keep solid boundaries, and care about me as a human while they do it.

Other creatives who support me, PF, and our clients and thereby inspire more creativity on a daily basis, including Ross Coverdale, who never fails to cheerfully review my latest and greatest idea with energy, strategy, and practicality; Col Gray, who has taught me more about branding than anyone else and who listens like a human and never rushes the process; Alasdair McGill, who gave me a new perspective on creativity by pointing out the impact of education and helped me understand a little more about design thinking and service design.

And last but by no means least: you the reader. You picked up this book, and if you're an accountant, that's a massive step on its own. Now that you've read it, I trust you are beginning to believe in, or are reigniting, your own creativity. It's inherent to you: It's not a faraway thing, only available to certain talented people. You are the talent. The only qualifications are that you be human (slightly more rare these days!) and that you lean into it, even when (especially when) you don't feel like it.

Keep dreaming, keep working, and keep trusting the creative process.

I will too.

ABOUT THE AUTHOR

Photo by The Profitable Firm (PF)

Karen L. Reyburn is a qualified accountant and founder of The Profitable Firm, a creative agency serving accountants worldwide. For over twenty years, she's helped accountants attract clients they love through a creative, structured approach to marketing. She lives on an island off the west coast of Scotland, where she's fueled by daily nature walks, strong black coffee, and the occasional dram of whisky with a good book. Visit karenlreyburn.com.

www.ingramcontent.com/pod-product-compliance
Lightning Source LLC
Chambersburg PA
CBHW050525240926
51846CB00003B/698
* 9 7 8 1 9 7 2 9 9 2 0 3 6 *